Let's Cook Japanese Food!

AMY KANEKO

Photography **Aubrie Pick**

weldon**owen**

Contents

TOFU & EGGS

VEGETABLES

RICE & NOODLES

Let's Cook Japanese Food!

What's a nice girl from New Jersey doing writing a Japanese cookbook? Quite simply, I wanted to share my experience of the delicious and easy everyday meals that I encountered in Japan with my friends and family here in North America.

I decided to live in Japan in my 20s on a whim—it appealed to my sense of adventure. So I took a couple of language classes and took off for Tokyo. I knew little of Japanese cuisine other than sushi. As a low-paid conversational English teacher, my meal budget didn't include high-end sushi, so I started to explore the full range of Japanese dishes. Tokyo has a tremendous selection of all kinds of food. I tried it all.

That first year, I subsisted on a lot of takeout and found a few local restaurants where the owners got to know me and delighted in sharing new foods with me to see how I'd react. There were few things that I found too strange to try—tentacles, grilled eel, fermented soybeans, fish eggs, unfamiliar root vegetables—you name it, I ate it. And loved it. Among the things I ate most often were the Japanese versions of Western-style foods, like hamburger, curry, fried cutlets, eggs, and more—things that I didn't know were really common in modern Japanese diets and just as Japanese as sushi.

Upon returning to New York, I missed these dishes and began watching the Japanese cable TV channel to get recipes. I moved to San Francisco for a job, and there I connected with a friend of one of my English conversation students, Shohei, who became my husband. He was transferred to Tokyo for work, and I went along. My Japanese coworkers and new in-laws were terrifically helpful in encouraging my Japanese food habit, patiently showing me ingredients, teaching me recipes, and introducing me to new dishes.

When Shohei and I moved back to San Francisco, I wanted to keep cooking Japanese food for him, and then later, when we had kids, for all of us. We now eat Japanese food at home at least three days a week and usually the type of dishes found in this book. I am happy to share these recipes and stories in the hope that you, too, will become a fan of Japanese cooking and will integrate it into your meals and parties. With this book, you will soon be cooking Japanese food with ease! I hope you love it. *Itadakimasu* (let's eat)!

— AMY KANEKO

Getting Started

There are a few basics that you might want to keep on hand so you can cook from this book anytime. Stock your kitchen with the items in the Shopping List below and you will be ready to make most of the recipes in this book. I've also provided a detailed list of everything you'll need in the Ingredients section (page 156). A primer on deep-frying, along with the recipe notes throughout the book, will help you learn essential cooking techniques.

日本 料理 頑張ってください! (Good luck and try hard to cook Japanese food!)

LEARNING HOW TO DEEP-FRY, JAPANESE STYLE

Many cooks are afraid of deep-frying, viewing it as difficult and messy, and many eaters imagine that the food will be greasy. If you follow a few easy rules, frying can be simple and neat—correctly prepared Japanese deep-fried foods are never oily, but light and crispy.

Set up a workstation with the flour, egg, and panko for breading the food lined up in their order of use. A wok or a deep, wide saucepan works well. Have a pair of long cooking chopsticks or tongs, a slotted spoon, or a spatula handy for transferring ingredients in and out of the pan safely and with a minimum of splashing. A deep-frying thermometer keeps track of the temperature of the oil, but if you don't have one, here is a simple test that you can use whenever you are deep-frying: When you think the oil is hot, hold a wooden chopstick upright in it. If small bubbles form immediately around the chopstick, the oil is ready. Use a wire rack for draining (paper towels are an easy alternative), and a small skimmer is handy for scooping stray fried bits out of the oil so they don't burn.

Always deep-fry food in small batches. If you crowd the pan, the oil temperature will drop, causing the foods to absorb the oil. After you remove a batch from the pan, check that the oil has returned to the correct temperature before you fry the next batch or the food will be greasy.

SHOPPING LIST: MUST HAVES

- Chili bean paste
- Dashi
- Mirin
- Miso
- Panko
- Rice
- Rice vinegar
- Sake
- Sesame oil
- Soy sauce
- Sugar
- Tonkatsu sauce
- Worcestershire sauce

FREQUENTLY USED INGREDIENTS

- Cornstarch
- English or Japanese Cucumber
- Eggs
- Eggplants
- Ginger
- Garlic
- Green onions
- Ground beef, chicken, and pork
- Kabocha pumpkin
- Onions (yellow)
- Tomato ketchup
- Tofu

Equipment

Equipment needs for cooking these recipes are undemanding. A few specialized tools, such as a rice cooker (which I highly recommend) and a mandoline, make some of the common tasks of Japanese cooking a little easier, but most tasks can be accomplished with the same everyday equipment you use for cooking Western meals.

Chopsticks: Found in Japanese restaurants everywhere, chopsticks *(ohashi)* seem to make your Japanese food taste better and more authentic. They come in many materials— bamboo and other wood, plastic, metal—and styles and in a range of prices, with prized *hinoki-* wood chopsticks at the top of the pile. Chopsticks in any style will accomplish their main task of ferrying your delicious cooking from bowl to mouth. *Waribashi* (disposable wooden chopsticks) are inexpensive and can be bought by the pack.

Long cooking chopsticks, once you get the hang of working with them, are the best tools for turning hot foods, especially when frying.

At a place setting, *ohashi* should be laid horizontally on the table below the main plate, with tips facing left for a right-handed person and right for a left-handed person. The tips are often placed on a chopstick rest—a small, decorated stand made of ceramic or other material. Keep in mind the following rules of etiquette, too: never leave your chopsticks stuck straight up in a bowl of rice, and don't use them to pass food to others, chopsticks to chopsticks, because both recall funeral customs. Also, never point with your chopsticks or spear your food with them. It's just not nice.

Drop-Lid: Known as an *otoshi-buta*, this wooden lid, which has a small wooden handle on top, fits just inside of a pot rim. It floats directly on top of the simmering foods, keeping them from moving around, helping to spread the flavors of the liquid evenly, and preventing the liquid from cooking away. *Nimono* (simmered) dishes such as *Otoosan no Kabocha Nimono* (page 59) and *Iridori* (page 135) employ this specialized lid. I make my own by shaping a disk of aluminum foil, which works passably well, except that you have to remember to use a potholder when fishing it out at the end of cooking, as it gets very hot. An Asian kitchen supplies store or website will have drop-lids in different sizes to fit your pots or you can improvise, as I do.

Grater: An inexpensive grater *(oroshi)* is used for preparing ginger and daikon. The graters come with different-sized rasps, depending on what you are grating. Many of my recipes call for grated ginger, so the fine-rasp ginger grater, which comes in ceramic, metal, or plastic, is particularly useful. The ceramic one is especially nice because it has a moat around the edge that captures all of the tiny grated pieces and the valuable juice.

Mandoline: This kitchen device is great for slicing onions, potatoes, cucumbers, and cabbage very thin with little effort. There are expensive mandolines on the market, but you can find inexpensive everyday slicers in well-stocked kitchenware stores. I often use the ceramic blade slicer made by Kyocera, especially when using a knife would be too tedious and the job is too small for my food processor. As with any slicer, be very careful to keep your fingers clear of the blade.

 Nabe: This earthenware cooking pot is traditionally used to make tabletop stews, such as *Sukiyaki* (page 151) and *Chankonabe* (page 138). If you have one, you can cook these dishes on your stove top and serve them at the table directly from the attractive clay pot (placed on a trivet, of course, to protect your tabletop). An enameled cast-iron pot, such as one from Le Creuset, will do as well.

 Rice Cooker: This is your most essential piece of kitchen equipment if you are planning to cook Japanese or other Asian dishes with any frequency. The electric rice cooker enables you to cook rice quickly and easily. Many of these "smart" machines adjust to the type of rice you're cooking (white, brown, recent harvest, older), the cooking method (steam, boil, make into gruel), and the time that you want to have the rice ready. You can set the cooker to start while you're still at work, and the rice will be done when you get home. Some rice cookers also have settings that will keep rice warm for use later in the day or even the next morning. Many are not too expensive, and even the most basic cooker usually turns out better rice, faster and more reliably, than the stove-top method.

 Suribachi: Nothing works better for grinding sesame seeds than a *suribachi*, a ceramic grinding bowl lined with ridges, and a wooden pestle *(surikogi)*—the Japanese version of the mortar and pestle. The bowl is glazed on the outside and unglazed on the inside. A coffee grinder that you use only for seeds and spices or a mini food processor also accomplishes the task. The *suribachi* is useful for preparing foods from other cuisines as well, such as pesto, and for combining ingredients to make salad dressings, crushing garlic, and more.

Wok: You can find woks for sale in most kitchenware shops, and you don't need to spend a lot of money to get a quality product. They come in a variety of materials, including carbon steel and anodized aluminum, and in both regular and nonstick finishes. Their rounded bottoms and high sloped sides make it easy to toss foods rapidly for stir-frying, though they are equally well suited to deep-frying and steaming. A 12-inch wok is a practical size for most kitchens.

Sauces

I don't want you to think that Japanese cooks create all of the sauces for modern Japanese dishes from scratch. In fact, just the opposite is the case. Bottled sauces for the most common dishes are in widespread use, and there is no shame in using them to achieve the right Japanese flavor. Some very simple flavorings are usually made from scratch, such as simmered liquids made from mirin, soy sauce, sugar, and sake, but prepared sauces save the day for Western-style dishes like *Yakisoba* (page 82), *Okonomiyaki* (page 30), *Tonkatsu* (page 110), and *Hamburg* (page 142). Many of these sauces are getting easier to find. The most commonly used sauces are included here.

Chili Bean Paste: Known as *toban djan*, this dark red paste contains bits of hot red chili, garlic, and mashed soybeans. Strong-flavored and spicy, it is frequently used in such Chinese-inspired recipes as *Mapo Dofu* (page 27), *Ebi no Chiri So-su* (page 107), and *Shohei no Butaniku to Goma Ramen* (page 91). It is hot, but not incendiary. Taste it before you use it to determine your own tolerance. Look for chili bean paste stocked alongside other Asian sauces in the international food aisle of most supermarkets. If you can't find it, chili garlic paste or chili garlic sauce can be substituted.

Goma Dare: This bottled sesame sauce, typically a mixture of sesame seeds, soy sauce, sugar, dashi, mirin, and other ingredients, is used straight from the bottle to dress steamed vegetables or as dipping sauce for *nabemono* (one-pot dishes).

Okonomiyaki Sauce: This sweet-sour-fruity combination of tomato, fruit, vinegar, and spices is closely related to *tonkatsu* sauce and *yakisoba* sauce, and in a pinch, any one of the three can be substituted for the others. If your regular market carries it, it will be stocked in the international food aisle along with other Asian sauces.

Oyster Sauce: Thick, salty, and slightly briny, this Chinese flavor waker-upper is combined with other sauces or used in small amounts on its own to enhance other flavors. Oyster sauce keeps well in the refrigerator after opening, and if the cap is cleaned and tightly closed after using, it will have a long life. It's found in the Chinese food section or with other Asian sauces in the international food aisle.

Ponzu Sauce: This bottled sauce combines citrus-flavored vinegar with soy sauce. The citrus fruit is traditionally yuzu, a type of citron, but versions using lemon, lime, or *sudachi* (a tiny Japanese lime) are also found in Japanese stores. The *ponzu* sauce found in most Western markets is fine for serving with the *Sukiyaki* on page 151, where the refreshing and cleansing bite of the citrus perfectly offsets the fatty richness of the meat. *Ponzu* can also be used as a seasoning for grilled or fried fish, or in salad dressings for a vinegary, citrusy kick.

Sukiyaki Sauce: You can purchase this sauce, which is used for cooking the dish, but it can also be made from scratch if you have soy sauce, mirin, and sugar on hand.

Teriyaki Sauce: This is probably the most popular Japanese sauce available outside of Japan. You can buy it in flavored versions, such as garlic. I've used only the regular flavor in my recipes. You can also make this one yourself. It's super easy (see the recipe for salmon on page 96 for a favorite version).

Tomato Ketchup: The tomatoey secret in countless Japanese dishes, Western ketchup, with its slightly sweet tomato taste, is a common ingredient in many of my recipes, either mixed with other ingredients or on its own. Kagome is the largest Japanese brand, but your usual will do.

Tonkatsu Sauce: Also called fruit sauce, this thick, slightly sweet, spiced (think cloves) sauce is indispensable in the modern Japanese kitchen. Bull Dog is a famous Japanese brand, but Kikkoman is the most widely available brand outside of Japan. Almost no one makes this sauce at home, so if you can't find it at your market, buy it online. It keeps in the refrigerator for a long time after opening.

Tsuyu: This sauce, which doubles as a soup base and a seasoning, is diluted for use as a broth for hot soba and udon or as a dipping sauce for soba and tempura. Most versions of *tsuyu* contain dashi, sake, soy sauce, and sometimes mirin or sugar. *Tentsuyu*, the classic dipping sauce for tempura, is a concentrated version of *tsuyu*, probably to balance the relatively strong flavor of the fried food. You can use a purchased sauce, diluting it as indicated on the bottle, if you don't want to make the homemade sauce that I have included with the tempura recipe on page 49. I have also included a homemade *tsuyu* sauce, milder than the tempura version, for dipping cold soba (page 87). A mild *tsuyu* is also recommended for *Agedashi Dofu* (page 24), but since you need only a small amount, a diluted bottled product is easiest.

Worcestershire Sauce: This British sauce is a major ingredient in Japan's Western-style recipes. Although thicker in texture, your favorite steak sauce can also work in a recipe calling for Worcestershire sauce. Just a little bit will perk up a dish.

Yakisoba Sauce: Yet another variation on the *tonkatsu*-sauce theme, bottled (or squeeze-bottled) *yakisoba* sauce is the way to go. It has an unmistakable tang and spice and gives the stir-fried noodle dish its distinctive flavor. You probably won't find it in your regular market, but you should seek it out online. It makes the dish and never fails to evoke memories of Japanese street fairs, where *yakisoba* is always sold.

HAMBURG SO-SU (HAMBURGER SAUCE)

Here are two versions, each making about 1¼ cups. One relies on bottled *tonkatsu* sauce and one you make from scratch. To make the sauce with bottled *tonkatsu* sauce: in a small saucepan over low to medium heat, combine 1 cup *tonkatsu* sauce, ¼ cup red wine, ¼ cup water, and 2 tablespoons ketchup, mix well, and cook about 3 minutes. To make the sauce from scratch: in a small saucepan over low to medium heat, combine 1 cup tomato ketchup, ¼ cup Worcestershire sauce, ¼ cup red wine, ¼ cup water, and 1 teaspoon sugar, mix well, and cook about 3 minutes. Store any leftover sauce in the refrigerator for up to 2 days. Use on hamburgers, meat loaf, or even on an omelet.

Tofu & Eggs

Tofu is a staple of the Japanese diet and is popular as a high-protein health food, and for its versatility. Until I lived in Japan, I didn't have a good idea of how to integrate tofu into my cooking. Once there, I saw how easy tofu is to use and discovered the wide variety of dishes that can be made with it.

Tofu is available in North America in three basic forms—soft, medium, and firm—and many regular markets stock at least two of them and sometimes all three. Soft, also called silken, is very soft, almost pudding-like, yet holds its shape, and is used for cold dishes like *Hiyayakko* (page 22) and in miso and other soups. The two firmer varieties hold their shape more easily without breaking, making them well suited to stir-fries and simmered dishes.

I have specified the tofu that I use or that is most commonly used in each recipe in this chapter, but for the most part, the texture that you like best will most likely work for all of the recipes.

Eggs are as versatile as tofu in Japanese cooking, turning up at every meal, rather than just at breakfast. Variations on the traditional omelet are practically a whole cuisine in themselves, plus a number of home-style dishes call for these inexpensive sources of high-quality protein for making batters, binding croquettes, coating food for frying, and more.

Eggs in Japan are a little different from those I was used to buying in the States. The first time I cracked open a Japanese egg I thought there was something wrong with it. Japanese eggs have dark yellow, nearly orange, yolks with a rich and rounded flavor. They're eaten all kinds of ways, from hard boiled to raw, and although I can't recommend you eat raw eggs because of the risk of salmonella bacteria, Japanese cooks regularly top bowls of hot rice or soup with raw eggs or use them as a dipping sauce for meat dishes, such as *Sukiyaki* (page 151).

Soft tofu is widely available, and the preparation of this simple classic is so easy. This dish is perfect for serving on a warm day and makes a wonderful light lunch with a salad or as an appetizer (as it is served in Japan). Young children love it too, since the tofu is soft and the taste mild. Soft tofu was my daughters' favorite food from the moment they started eating solids.

Cold Tofu with Ginger & Green Onions

4-inch cube soft tofu

1 tablespoon minced green onion, including tender green tops

About 1 teaspoon peeled and grated fresh ginger

About ½ teaspoon soy sauce

SERVES 1

1 Place the tofu in a shallow bowl. Sprinkle with the green onion and a small amount of grated ginger and drizzle with soy sauce, adding more ginger and soy sauce to taste.

note: *Hiyayakko* is usually made using soft tofu, but at some *izakaya*, where the dish is common, *momen* ("cotton" or firm) tofu is used. Use the type that you prefer. I have given the amounts of each ingredient for a single serving, which you can easily adjust to the number of diners, each with their own portion.

IZAKAYA An *izakaya* is the Japanese equivalent of the bar or pub, a place where people go for drinking and camaraderie—*Izakaya* are usually most crowded when salarymen get off work and convene there with their co-workers to let off steam. These casual spots also serve food to accompany the beer, sake, or *shochu* (a vodka-like spirit). Usually the food is a selection of small dishes, known collectively as *ippin ryori*, a sort of Japanese "tapas," such as *Hiyayakko, Kara-age* (page 123), potato salad (page 66), and simple pieces of grilled fish or meat, or sashimi (but never sushi).

A creamy interior and crispy coating make this fried tofu, paired with a salty-sweet-gingery sauce, a great appetizer. Use soft tofu and take the time to drain it before frying, as that will make it easier to work with. Firmer tofu can be used, but will be less delicate.

AGEDASHI DOFU

Fried Soft Tofu in Sweet Soy Sauce

1 package (14 ounces) soft tofu

Cornstarch for dusting

Canola or other neutral oil for deep-frying

2 green onions, including tender green tops, thinly sliced

2 teaspoons peeled and grated fresh ginger

¼ cup warmed *tsuyu* (page 17)

SERVES 2

1 Carefully remove the tofu from its package and cut it into 4 equal pieces. Place several layers of paper towels on a cutting board and place the tofu in a single layer on the towels. Top each tofu quarter with several paper towels, then top with a plate and a weight, such as a can of tomatoes. Let drain for 15 minutes, then very carefully replace all of the paper towels and let drain for another 15 minutes.

2 Pat the tofu dry and cut it into 2-inch squares. Pour some cornstarch into a small, shallow bowl and set near the stove. Place the tofu next to the cornstarch.

3 In a deep, wide saucepan, pour 3 inches of oil and heat to 350°F on a deep-frying thermometer or until bubbles immediately form around a wooden chopstick held upright in the pan. When the oil is ready, very gently dust 1 piece of tofu on all sides with the cornstarch and, using a flat spoon, carefully lower it into the hot oil. Repeat with more tofu, dusting the tofu just before frying and working in batches to avoid crowding. Fry the tofu until the coating is crispy and firm and lightly golden but not browned, 2–3 minutes. Using a slotted spatula, carefully transfer to paper towels to drain. Repeat until all the tofu is fried. (I usually serve warm as each batch is ready, but the tofu will stay warm for a few minutes.)

4 Divide the tofu evenly in individual bowls and top with the green onions and ginger. Pour some of the warm *tsuyu* into the bowls just before serving so that the tofu doesn't get soggy. Serve right away.

A popular and easy Japanese dish, *Gomoku Iridofu* can be served as a main course or as a side. The number five plays an important role in Japanese cuisine. A classic balanced meal traditionally includes five flavors, five types of food preparation, and five colors.

GOMOKU IRIDOFU

Tofu with "Five Things"

8-10 snow peas for garnish

3 fresh shiitake mushrooms

1 boneless, skinless chicken thigh

1 teaspoon canola or other neutral oil

1 small carrot, peeled and chopped

2 tablespoons chopped bamboo shoots

1 package (14 ounces) medium or firm tofu

1 tablespoon soy sauce

1½ teaspoons sugar

Pinch of salt

1 large egg, lightly beaten

2 green onions, including tender green tops, chopped

SERVES 4

1 Trim the snow peas. Have ready a bowl of ice water. Blanch the peas in boiling water for 1 minute, drain, and immerse in the ice water until chilled through. Drain again, cut into slivers diagonally, and reserve for garnish.

2 Remove and discard the mushroom stems and thinly slice the mushroom caps. Remove and discard any visible fat from the chicken thigh and cut the meat into ½-inch pieces.

3 In a large saucepan over medium heat, warm the oil until hot. Add the mushrooms, chicken, carrot, and bamboo shoots and cook, stirring, until the chicken just loses its pink color, about 3 minutes. Drain the tofu and add whole to the pan. Using a wooden spoon or spatula, break up the tofu into large chunks. Stir in the soy sauce, sugar, and salt, then add the egg. Continue to stir, breaking up the tofu into smaller pieces, until the egg has set in small pieces and is well incorporated. Check that the vegetables are tender and the chicken cooked through, then add the green onions and mix one more time.

4 Garnish with the snow peas and serve piping hot.

note: To make this recipe vegetarian, replace the chicken with another type of mushroom.

Mapo Dofu is one of the staple dishes found in Chinese restaurants in Japan as well as in home kitchens. Chinese-inspired recipes are very popular in contemporary Japanese cuisine, and this spicy, hearty dish makes an excellent family dinner.

MAPO DOFU

Spicy Tofu with Minced Pork

FOR THE SAUCE

2 teaspoons chili bean paste

½ cup chicken broth

1 teaspoon oyster sauce

1 tablespoon soy sauce

1 tablespoon sake

1 teaspoon sugar

2 teaspoons cornstarch dissolved in 2 teaspoons water

About 1 teaspoon sesame oil

6 green onions

3 cloves garlic, minced

1-inch piece fresh ginger, peeled and minced

2 tablespoons canola or other neutral oil

½ pound ground pork

2 packages (14 ounces each) soft tofu, drained

3 cups hot cooked rice (see *Gohan*, page 73) for serving

SERVES 4

1 To make the sauce, in a small bowl, measure the chili bean paste. In another small bowl, stir together the broth, oyster sauce, soy sauce, sake, and sugar. Set the 2 bowls near the stove along with the cornstarch-water mixture and the bottle of sesame oil.

2 Mince the white parts and tender green tops of 4 green onions. Mince the white parts of the remaining 2 green onions, then halve the tender green tops lengthwise and slice them crosswise into 1-inch-wide pieces. Place the minced green onions, garlic, and ginger in 3 separate bowls. Reserve the sliced green onion tops for garnish.

3 Heat a wok or frying pan over high heat until hot. Add the canola oil and swirl the pan to coat the bottom and sides with oil. When the oil is very hot, add the minced green onions and garlic, stir well, and reduce the heat to medium before the garlic scorches. Add the ground pork and, using a spatula, continue to stir constantly, breaking up the pork. When the pork is just cooked, about 2 minutes, add the chili bean paste and pour in the broth mixture. Mix the ingredients with the sauce until well combined.

4 Place the tofu in the pan. Using the edge of the spatula, cut it into large chunks and cook until the tofu is heated through, about 2 minutes. Stir the cornstarch-water mixture, then pour it slowly into the pan, stirring until the sauce in the pan thickens, about 1 minute. Drizzle in a little sesame oil.

5 Spoon into a serving bowl, garnish with the reserved green onion slices, and serve with individual bowls of rice.

At most Japanese restaurants in the States, a set meal invariably begins with a small bowl of this iconic soup. (In Japan, miso soup is traditionally served at the end of the meal.) In too many places, the *miso shiru* is the product of an inexpensive packet that holds the entire soup, minus the liquid, in desiccated form. Making your own miso soup is very easy!

MISO SHIRU

Miso Soup

3 cups dashi (page 156)

¼ cup miso, preferably white miso

½ block soft tofu, about 7 ounces, cut into ½-inch cubes

2 green onions, including tender green tops, minced

Pinch of dried *wakame* seaweed, reconstituted (see note; optional)

SERVES 4

1 In a small saucepan, bring the dashi to a boil. Reduce the heat so that the dashi simmers. To prevent the miso from forming salty lumps in your soup, put 1 tablespoon of miso into a large spoon and, holding the spoon in one hand and a pair of chopsticks in the other, dip the edge of the spoon into the hot broth, scooping up a little of it onto the spoon. Holding the spoon above the broth, stir together the miso and dashi with the chopsticks to dissolve the miso, and then add the dissolved miso to the simmering broth. Repeat with the rest of the miso.

2 When the miso has been mixed in, add the tofu and heat through, about 1 minute. Add the green onions and the *wakame* (if using) and cook for 30 seconds longer, making sure the soup does not boil.

3 Divide the soup among 4 bowls and serve piping hot.

note: *Wakame,* a type of seaweed recognized for its healthful nutrients and used primarily in soups and salads, is almost always sold dried. To reconstitute it, soak it in warm water for 20–30 minutes, rinse, and add to your dish.

Tamago Toji Jiru is the first—and easiest—recipe that *okaasan* (my mother-in-law) shared with me, after we had eaten it at breakfast one morning. Even *okaasan* uses *dashi-no-moto,* or instant dashi, rather than preparing dashi from scratch. Serve this soup at any meal of the day. This recipe is for a single serving, but you can multiply it to accommodate any number of diners.

TAMAGO TOJI JIRU

Stirred Egg Soup

1 green onion

1 medium egg

1 cup dashi (page 156) or chicken broth

½ teaspoon sake

Pinch of salt

⅛ teaspoon sesame oil (optional)

SERVES 1

1 Halve the green onion lengthwise, then slice crosswise into 1-inch-wide pieces. Set aside.

2 Break the egg into a small bowl, beat lightly just until blended, and set aside. In a small saucepan over medium heat, bring the dashi to a rolling simmer. Add the sake and salt. Then, using chopsticks or a fork, stir the egg into the dashi and swirl the pan for about 30 seconds so the egg sets in long threads. Remove from the heat.

3 Drizzle in the sesame oil for aroma, if you like. Pour into a bowl and serve right away, topped with the green onion.

Okonomiyaki, literally "grilled as you like it," originated in Osaka. A popular group meal, it is often served with *Yakisoba* (page 82), and Hiroshima-style *Okonomiyaki* marries the two into a sort of noodle-filled pancake. It's easy to prepare at home and a real crowd-pleaser, for kids and drinking buddies alike.

OKONOMIYAKI

"As You Like It" Savory Pancake

10 slices thick-cut bacon

5 or 6 shrimp

1 cup all-purpose flour

½ teaspoon baking powder

Pinch of salt

2 large eggs

½ medium head green cabbage, coarsely chopped

1 green onion, including tender green top, thinly sliced

4 tablespoons canola or other neutral oil

1 cup *Okonomiyaki* (page 16) or *Tonkatsu* sauce (page 17), warmed, for serving

¼ cup mayonnaise for serving

Aonori (page 161) and *katsuobushi* (see note) for serving

SERVES 2

1 Place the bacon in a single layer between 2 layers of paper towels and microwave on high for 3 minutes until cooked through but not crispy, or cook the bacon in a frying pan over medium-high heat, turning as needed, 4-5 minutes. Cut each slice into several pieces. Boil the shrimp until cooked through, about 3 minutes. Drain, peel, and cut into ½-inch pieces.

2 In a large bowl, using a fork or chopsticks, stir together the flour, baking powder, salt, and 1 cup minus 1 tablespoon water. Beat in the eggs until well mixed. Stir in the cabbage, green onion, bacon, and shrimp.

3 Heat a 10-inch nonstick frying pan over medium-high heat until hot, add 2 tablespoons of the oil and swirl to coat the bottom of the pan. When the oil is hot, use a ladle to pour half the batter into the pan to create a large pancake. Cook, without disturbing, until just browned on the bottom, about 5 minutes. When the pancake can slide easily on the pan (don't be tempted to flip it before it has set!), use a spatula to carefully flip it and cook it on the second side until lightly browned, 4-5 minutes longer. Transfer the pancake to a plate and repeat with the remaining 2 tablespoons oil and batter to make one more.

4 Meanwhile, place the sauce, mayonnaise, *aonori*, and *katsuobushi* in small separate bowls on the table. To serve, drizzle on the sauce and mayonnaise, and then top with *aonori* and *katsuobushi*. If the sauce is properly hot, the *katsuobushi* will seem to dance.

note: *Katsuobushi,* the same dried bonito flakes used for making dashi from scratch, is also the traditional topping for *Hiyayakko* (page 22), *Yakisoba* (page 82), and *yudofu* (simmered tofu). Most commonly sold in small individual packets in a box or bag, the bonito can be stored in a cupboard until used.

TAKOYAKI *Takoyaki,* a specialty of Osaka and Kyoto, is a bite-sized variation of *okonomiyaki.* The same basic batter (minus the cabbage and other additions) is cooked in a special pan with round molds about 2 inches in diameter. The batter is poured into each well and then a small piece of boiled octopus *(tako)* and perhaps a little green onion and a few small pieces of *beni shoga* (bright pink pickled ginger) are poked into the center. When the bottoms have solidified, each ball is carefully lifted with a toothpick and flipped to the other side to cook, resulting in a perfect, golf ball–sized sphere. When the *takoyaki* are done, the outside is pancake-like and crisp, while the inside is soft and almost molten—a delicious contrast. *Takoyaki* are served in little paper trays of six pieces, and they are garnished with the same sauces, plus *aonori* and *katsuobushi,* as on *okonomiyaki.* It is tempting to eat them immediately, but be aware that the inside of freshly cooked *takoyaki* is very hot! They are a common sight at street festivals and at *yatai* (street-food stalls). My favorite time to eat them is at the New Year, after my husband, his extended family, our children, and I have all made the long, cold trek to the local shrine for the traditional New Year's blessing. On the walk back, we always pass a *takoyaki* stand, and the piping hot snacks are the perfect treat.

This is one of the classic Japanese *yoshoku* dishes, very quick to make and exceptionally tasty. Some places in Tokyo serve nothing but this dish and offer different rice-based fillings and toppings, such as curry sauce (page 147) or *Hayashi* beef sauce (page 144) spooned over the top.

OMU RAISU

Omelet Stuffed with Tomatoey Chicken Rice

FOR THE FILLING

1 tablespoon unsalted butter

1 boneless, skinless chicken thigh, cut into ½-inch pieces

¼ cup chopped white mushrooms

½ yellow onion, minced

1½ cups cooked rice (see *Gohan*, page 73), cold or at room temperature

¼ cup tomato ketchup, plus more for garnish

¼ cup chicken broth

Salt and freshly ground pepper

1 To make the filling, in a large frying pan over medium heat, melt ½ tablespoon of the butter. When the butter is hot, add the chicken and cook, stirring often, until the chicken is half cooked, about 2 minutes. Add the mushrooms and cook, stirring often, until the chicken is cooked through and the mushrooms are tender, 2–3 minutes longer. Transfer to a bowl and set aside.

2 Return the pan to medium heat and melt the remaining ½ tablespoon butter. Add the onion and cook, stirring often, until translucent, about 5 minutes. Add the rice and, using a wooden spatula, press against it to separate the grains. Cook for about 1 minute, stirring to prevent sticking, then add the ketchup, broth, and chicken mixture. Mix well and cook until all the liquid is absorbed, about 3 minutes. Season with ½ teaspoon salt and a few grinds of pepper, remove from the heat, and keep warm.

3 To make the first omelet, in a bowl, crack 3 of the eggs, add 1 tablespoon of the milk and ¼ teaspoon of the salt, and beat with a fork or chopsticks until well blended.

Continued on page 38

1 Lift the edges of the eggs occasionally to allow even cooking.

2 When the eggs are mostly set, add the filling.

3 Fold the omelet over the filling completely.

FOR THE OMELETS

6 large eggs

2 tablespoons whole or low-fat milk

½ teaspoon salt

1 tablespoon unsalted butter

2 sprigs fresh parsley for garnish (optional)

SERVES 2

Continued from page 37

The omelet should still be soft in the middle when the filling is added, and then it should be carefully flipped over the filling, so that each diner is presented with a football-shaped yellow omelet topped with a squiggle of ketchup and a sprig of parsley. The texture of the soft egg combined with the tomatoey rice is sublime. *Omu Raisu* is eaten with a spoon.

4 In a 10-inch omelet pan or nonstick frying pan over medium heat, melt ½ tablespoon of the butter. When the foam subsides, add the egg mixture and swirl the pan to spread it evenly. Using a fork, scramble quickly for about 30 seconds and then swirl the pan again so the eggs coat the entire bottom. Continue to cook, lifting the edges of the eggs occasionally to allow the uncooked portion to flow underneath. When the eggs are mostly set and just a little wet on top, 3–4 minutes, place half of the filling on half of the omelet, then tip the pan (or use chopsticks to help) so that the omelet folds over the filling completely and slide the finished omelet, using a spatula, onto a plate.

5 Cover the omelet with a paper towel and pinch in the ends with your hands, gently shaping it into a football shape if you can. If the omelet is not perfectly shaped, don't worry! It will still be delicious. Keep the omelet warm while you repeat the steps to make the second omelet with the remaining ingredients. Top each omelet with a squiggle of ketchup and garnish with a parsley sprig, if desired. Serve hot.

This large, fluffy crab omelet with a savory gravy is an example of Japanese home-style cooking borrowed liberally from Chinese cuisine (*chuka ryori*) and refashioned to Japanese taste. The soft eggs make the omelet a perfect topping for a rice bowl (*donburi*).

KANITAMA

Chinese-Style Crab Omelet with Soy Sauce Gravy

4 large eggs

Pinch of salt

½ cup fresh or canned crabmeat

2 tablespoons slivered bamboo shoots (optional)

2 green onions, including tender green tops, minced

2 fresh shiitake mushrooms, stems removed and caps thinly sliced

2 tablespoons frozen peas

FOR THE GRAVY

½ cup chicken broth

1½ teaspoons soy sauce

1½ teaspoons sugar

¼ teaspoon sake

Pinch of salt

1½ teaspoons cornstarch dissolved in 1½ teaspoons water

2 tablespoons canola or other neutral oil

½ teaspoon sesame oil

SERVES 2

1 Break the eggs into a large bowl, beat with a fork or chopsticks until well blended, and stir in the salt. Pick over the crabmeat for shell fragments and cartilage. Add the crabmeat, bamboo shoots (if using), green onions, mushrooms, and peas to the eggs and mix thoroughly. Set aside.

2 To make the gravy, in a small saucepan over medium heat, combine the chicken broth, soy sauce, sugar, sake, and salt and bring just to a simmer. Stir the cornstarch-water mixture, then pour it slowly into the pan and cook, stirring, until thickened, 1–2 minutes. Keep the gravy warm.

3 Heat a wok or frying pan over high heat until hot. Add the canola oil and swirl the pan to coat the bottom and sides with oil. When the oil is very hot, add the egg mixture. When it sizzles as it hits the pan, quickly add the sesame oil and, using a spatula, stir the egg mixture constantly, lifting and pushing the edges so the uncooked portion flows underneath. When the omelet is completely cooked but still soft, pile it in the center of the pan and let the bottom cook briefly, until the mass is solidified, the top is still quite soft, and the bottom is lightly browned, 1–2 minutes. Slide the omelet in two portions either over a bowl of rice or into a large, shallow bowl and ladle the warm sauce over the top. Eat with a spoon.

This is a classic starter: part soup and part custard, a savory pudding with small bites of chicken, shiitake, and other little surprises. My daughter Nami is the expert *chawanmushi* maker in our house. The additions are accents, thought of as treasures in the custardy base.

CHAWANMUSHI

Savory Egg Custard

1 teaspoon canola or other neutral oil

1 teaspoon sake

½ boneless, skinless chicken thigh cut into bite-sized pieces, and just cooked through with a little oil and a teaspoon of sake in a frying pan

2 eggs

1 cup dashi (page 156) or chicken broth

Pinch of salt

½ teaspoon soy sauce

1 teaspoon mirin

1½ tablespoons slivered bamboo shoots (optional)

2 small fresh shiitake mushrooms, stems removed and caps thinly sliced

1 green onion, including tender green top, chopped

4 cooked, peeled, and deveined shrimp, sliced in half lengthwise

4 snow peas, trimmed (optional)

4 sprigs fresh parsley or cilantro for garnish (optional)

SERVES 4

1 Fill a large pot with 3 inches of water and bring to a boil.

2 Meanwhile, in a frying pan over medium heat, warm the oil with the sake, add the chicken, and cook until the chicken is just cooked through, about 4 minutes. Set aside.

3 In a large bowl, whisk the eggs, dashi, and salt. For a silky custard, strain the egg mixture into another bowl through a sieve. Using the back of a spoon, press the liquid through the sieve to extract as much egg as possible. Stir in the soy sauce and mirin and set aside.

4 Evenly divide the chicken, bamboo shoots (if using), mushrooms, green onion, shrimp, and snow peas among 4 small ramekins or heat-safe cups. Fill each ramekin three-fourths full with the egg mixture. Cover each ramekin very tightly with aluminum foil. Gently place them into the pot of boiling water so the water reaches about halfway up the sides of the ramekins without letting water get into the custards. Reduce the heat and barely simmer, covered, until a wooden skewer or chopstick inserted into the center of a custard comes out clean and the custards appear set, 10–15 minutes.

5 Carefully remove the ramekins from the water. To serve hot, uncover and garnish each custard with a parsley sprig, if desired. To serve cold, let cool, and refrigerate until chilled through before garnishing with parsley, if desired.

note: Try to keep the water temperature at a simmer because if the water boils, the custard may develop bubbles instead of setting with a smooth surface.

Vegetables

I'm always looking for ways to get more vegetables into my family's diet. In Japanese cuisine, vegetables are not just an afterthought at the side of the plate. Instead, they often occupy several of the little plates that are served with every meal. My father-in-law takes pride in the small garden in front of his house in Japan, and the daikon and other vegetables that he grows there and stores in the back shed are often part of a meal. When I lived in Tokyo, I loved to shop at the local *yao-ya* (vegetable store), where the proprietor would give me suggestions on what to cook and how to cook it. One thing that I learned right away about vegetable shopping in Japan is that I was not to touch the produce on display. Rather, I was to point to my choice and let the clerk pick it up and hand it to me. It is no wonder that the displays of vegetables and fruits in Japan are so perfect.

These recipes aren't vegetarian, but vegetables are the focus of the dish. A little meat is often added to these dishes to enhance them, but the vegetables remain the stars. In general, Japanese like their vegetables cooked or pickled, rather than raw or in salads, and this chapter reflects that tradition.

This is the classic Japanese salad. My mother-in-law—along with many older Japanese—believes that eating vegetables raw isn't good for you. The volume of the raw vegetables makes you think that you are eating a lot of vegetables but actually you are not. She either cooks or marinates vegetables so that you are inclined to eat more of them.

SUNOMONO

Cucumber & Shrimp Salad with Vinegar Dressing

1 English cucumber, halved lengthwise, seeded (if any), and sliced paper thin

½ teaspoon salt

½ pound small shrimp, peeled, deveined, and halved lengthwise

¼ cup rice vinegar

1 tablespoon sugar

½ teaspoon soy sauce

SERVES 4 AS A SIDE DISH

1 Place the cucumber slices in a colander set over a large bowl, sprinkle with the salt, and let stand for 30 minutes.

2 Meanwhile, bring a saucepan filled with water to a boil, add the shrimp, and cook until they turn pink and begin to curl, about 3 minutes. Drain, immediately rinse under running cold water to halt the cooking, and set aside.

3 In a small bowl, stir together the vinegar, sugar, and soy sauce until the sugar is dissolved.

4 Rinse the salt off the cucumber slices. Using your hands, squeeze them several times to extract as much water as possible. Pat the cucumber dry with paper towels and place in a bowl. Add the shrimp and pour over the vinegar mixture. Using your hands, mix the ingredients well, cover, and refrigerate for at least 30 minutes to allow the flavors to meld.

5 Serve the salad cold or at room temperature.

While I grew up eating a heavy Eastern European–style stuffed cabbage, Mayumi, my sister-in-law, introduced me to her *sappari* (light) version, stuffed with pork and shrimp and served in chicken broth rather than a rich tomato sauce.

MAYUMI NO RORU CABEGI

Mayumi's Cabbage Rolls

1 head green cabbage

5 green onions, including tender green tops, thinly sliced

2 slices white bread, torn into small pieces

¼ pound shrimp, peeled, deveined, and cut into small pieces

¼ pound ground pork

1½ teaspoons ginger juice (page 157)

Salt and freshly ground pepper

1 tablespoon sake

5 cups chicken broth

¼ cup tomato ketchup

5 tablespoons mayonnaise

SERVES 4

1 Fill a large pot three-fourths full of water and bring to a boil. Add the whole cabbage, submerging it in the water. When the water returns to a boil, transfer the cabbage to a colander to drain, reserving about 6 tablespoons of the cooking water for the sauce.

2 When the cabbage is cool enough to handle, carefully peel off at least 8 large leaves without tears or heavy spines and place them on paper towels to drain.

3 In a bowl, combine the green onions, bread, shrimp, pork, ginger juice, ½ teaspoon salt, ¼ teaspoon pepper, and the sake. Using your hands, mix the ingredients until well combined.

4 In a large saucepan over medium-high heat, bring the chicken broth to a gentle boil. Meanwhile, position a cabbage leaf with the stem facing you. Place 2-3 tablespoons of the filling in the middle of the leaf, fold in both sides, bring the edge nearest you over the filling to cover it, roll up, and secure the roll with a toothpick, being careful not to tear the cabbage leaf. Repeat to make 7 or more rolls, depending on how much filling and how many leaves you have.

While I love to eat the rolls hot in the soup in which they are cooked, they are also good at room temperature, sliced and drizzled with a little of the ketchup-and-mayonnaise sauce. Make the rolls on the smallish side, so they are easier to handle and cook quickly.

1 Place filling in the middle of the leaf.

2 Fold in both sides.

3 Roll the leaf away from you.

4 Secure the roll with a toothpick.

5 When the broth is slowly boiling, carefully place the cabbage rolls in the pan, arranging most of the rolls in a single layer with 1 or 2 rolls on top. Cover the pan with a drop-lid (page 11) and cook until the cabbage leaves are very tender, easily pierced with a fork or chopstick, but not disintegrating, 30–35 minutes. Season the broth to taste with salt.

6 Meanwhile, in a small bowl, stir together the ketchup, 3 tablespoons of the reserved cabbage cooking water, and the mayonnaise until well blended. If needed, use the remaining 3 tablespoons cooking water to make more sauce.

7 To serve as a main course, place 2 cabbage rolls each in 4 shallow bowls, add enough broth to reach about halfway up the sides of the rolls, and drizzle with the sauce. To serve as appetizers, divide the rolls, broth, and sauce among 8 bowls. Serve right away.

Tempura is, of course, popular in the West, so I had eaten it many times before my first visit to Japan. When I arrived in Tokyo, I discovered that, like teriyaki, tempura in its homeland is quite different from its Western counterpart.

YASAI TO EBI TEMPURA

Vegetable & Shrimp Tempura

Canola or other neutral oil for deep-frying

2 tablespoons sesame oil (optional)

FOR THE BATTER

Ice cubes

1 cup all-purpose flour, sifted

1½ cups ice water

1 large egg

Pinch of salt

FOR THE DIPPING SAUCE

1 cup plus 1 tablespoon dashi (page 156) or water

⅓ cup mirin

⅓ cup soy sauce

4-8 large shrimp, peeled and deveined with tails intact

1 yellow onion, cut into ½-inch-thick slices

¼ small *kabocha* pumpkin, seeded and cut into ¼-inch-thick unpeeled slices

1 Pour the canola oil to a depth of 3 inches into a wok or deep, wide saucepan, add the sesame oil (if using), and heat to 350°F on a deep-frying thermometer or until bubbles immediately form around a wooden chopstick held upright in the pan.

2 Meanwhile, make the batter. Fill a large bowl with the ice cubes, and then nest a second bowl in the cubes. Add the flour, ice water, egg, and salt to the second bowl and, using a fork or chopsticks, stir lightly just until all the flour is moistened, the egg is incorporated, and the batter is lumpy, rather than smooth. Place near the stove.

3 To make the dipping sauce, in a small saucepan, heat the dashi over medium-low heat. Add the mirin and soy sauce, stir to mix, remove from the heat, and keep warm. Have the daikon and ginger ready.

4 Ready the shrimp, onion, pumpkin, sweet potato, and eggplant and place near the stove.

5 When the oil is ready, using tongs or chopsticks, pick up 1 piece to be fried, dip it briefly into the batter, coating it only lightly, and carefully drop it into the hot oil. Working in batches to avoid crowding, repeat with a few more pieces (this process could take a while, but crowding results in steaming rather than crisping). As the foods fry, use a slotted spoon or wire skimmer to remove bits

Continued on page 50

Continued from page 49

In Japan, where some of the finest restaurants specialize in the dish, I was introduced to tempura that was as light as air and had a melt-in-your-mouth crispiness. The secret to good tempura lies in the high-quality ingredients, a thin batter, and attentive frying.

1 sweet potato, peeled and cut into ¼-inch-thick slices

1 Japanese or Chinese eggplant, trimmed, halved crosswise and lengthwise into ¼-inch-thick slices

About ¼ cup grated daikon (page 156) for serving

About 2 tablespoons peeled and grated fresh ginger for serving

SERVES 2

of fried batter floating in the oil. Fry until the coating is crispy and still light colored but not browned, 3–4 minutes for most foods (for pumpkin and sweet potato, lower the heat slightly so they do not color too much as they fry longer). Using chopsticks or the slotted spoon or skimmer, transfer the pieces to a wire rack or paper towels to drain.

6 To serve, divide the warm dipping sauce between 2 small bowls and divide the daikon and ginger between 2 small plates for diners to mix to taste into their sauce bowls. Serve the tempura right away.

🌼 **note:** This batter is almost watery and lumps of flour are encouraged. If it is too well stirred, you will end up with a gummy, thick, floury coating that will absorb too much oil as it fries. Use a large pot, keep the oil at a steady heat, fry no more than a few pieces at the same time, and constantly skim off any errant bits of batter from the oil.

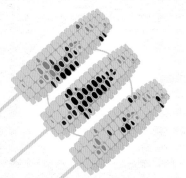

When corn is cooked over a fire, the kernels brown and caramelize, becoming absolutely delicious. My husband introduced me to "Japanese" corn on the cob: simply grilled and sweet, balanced by the salty soy sauce. No butter is needed. And as with many of the discoveries I made in learning about his cuisine, his way is a keeper.

CORN SHOYU-YAKI

Grilled Corn on the Cob

4 ears corn, shucked

Soy sauce

SERVES 4

1 Prepare a hot fire in a charcoal or gas grill, or preheat the broiler.

2 If using a grill, place the corn directly over the fire and grill, turning as needed, until the kernels are slightly charred or darkened, 5–7 minutes. If using a broiler, position the rack as close as possible to the heat source, arrange the corn on a broiler pan, and broil, turning as needed, about 15 minutes.

3 Transfer the hot corn to a platter, season to taste with soy sauce, and serve.

note: Outdoor grilling is uncommon in Japan, as few homes have backyard space for the necessary equipment. Despite that, *yakimono,* or "grilled foods," is a key part of the national cuisine. Most meals include a grilled dish, whether eating out or at home. Restaurants specializing in eel *kabayaki* are smoky places where eel is continually basted in a sweet sauce as it cooks on large grills. At a *yakitori-ya,* grilled skewered chicken is the specialty, showcasing all parts of the bird, from the thigh meat to the hearts. At *robata-yaki* and *teppan yaki* establishments, all kinds of foods—meats, seafood, vegetables—are cooked on a grill or on a griddle, respectively. Finally, at *yakiniku* (literally, "grilled meat") places, customers grill their own meals. In a Western kitchen, similar results can be achieved using a gas or charcoal grill outside, or even a standard oven broiler.

A crunchy mix of vegetables and savory bits of pork simply stir-fried over high heat, this is a great way to use up leftovers. College kids cook this in their dorms, it's found at lunch counters and restaurants, and busy moms make it for their families.

YASAI ITAME

Stir-fried Vegetables with Pork

½ green bell pepper, halved and seeded

Salt and freshly ground pepper

1 large carrot, peeled, cut crosswise into thirds, and thinly sliced lengthwise

6 slices thick-cut bacon, cut into 1-inch pieces

1 tablespoon canola or other neutral oil

1 small yellow onion, cut into ¼-inch-thick slices

4 fresh shiitake mushrooms, stems removed and caps sliced (optional)

½ head green cabbage, chopped into 2-inch pieces

4 or 5 green onions, including tender green tops, cut into 2-inch lengths

½ cup bean sprouts, ends trimmed (optional)

½ teaspoon soy sauce

SERVES 4

1 Cut the bell pepper lengthwise into ¼-inch-wide strips, then halve the strips crosswise and set aside.

2 Fill a small saucepan with water and bring to a boil. Salt the water lightly, add the carrot, and blanch for 1 minute. Drain and immediately rinse under running cold water to halt the cooking. Set aside.

3 In a wok or large frying pan over high heat, cook the bacon, stirring until cooked through but not crisp, about 4 minutes. Using a slotted spoon, transfer to a bowl and set aside.

4 Pour out any fat from the pan. Wipe the pan clean and return to high heat. Add the oil, swirl to coat the bottom and sides, and heat until the oil is almost smoking. Add the bell pepper, yellow onion, mushrooms (if using), and carrot and stir-fry for 2–3 minutes. Add the cabbage, green onions, and bean sprouts (if using) and stir-fry for 2 minutes longer. Return the bacon to the pan and stir-fry for 1 minute. Check that all the vegetables are just barely tender. Season to taste with salt and pepper, drizzle with the soy sauce, and remove from the heat.

5 Transfer to a large platter and serve before the vegetables get soggy.

Kabocha, a pumpkin with edible green skin and bright orange flesh, makes a sweet, dense filling for *korokke.* I form these croquettes into spheres the size of golf balls just because they cook quicker and they look cute!

KABOCHA KOROKKE

Pumpkin Croquettes

½ *kabocha* pumpkin

About 2 cups chicken broth or water

1 tablespoon unsalted butter

½ yellow onion, minced

2 tablespoons soy sauce

2 tablespoons mayonnaise

Pinch of salt

¼ teaspoon freshly ground pepper

1 cup all-purpose flour

1 large egg

About 2 cups *panko* (page 161)

Canola or other neutral oil for deep-frying

Tonkatsu sauce (page 17) for serving

MAKES ABOUT 20 SMALL CROQUETTES

1 Seed the pumpkin and cut into 2-inch unpeeled chunks. In a saucepan over medium heat, combine the *kabocha* with the broth to cover, bring to a simmer, cover, and cook until the flesh and skin are soft enough to mash, 15–20 minutes.

2 Meanwhile, in a small frying pan over medium heat, melt the butter. When the butter foams, add the onion and cook, stirring often, until translucent, 4–5 minutes. Remove from the heat.

3 Drain the pumpkin well. Transfer to a large bowl and, using a potato masher or the back of a fork, mash until fairly smooth. Add the onion, soy sauce, mayonnaise, salt, and pepper and mix well. Let cool a bit.

4 Spread the flour in a small, shallow bowl. Break the egg into a second shallow bowl and beat with chopsticks or a fork until well blended. Spread about 1 cup of the *panko* in a third shallow bowl, refilling the bowl as needed. Spread a little *panko* on a flat plate.

5 Dampen your hands and form the pumpkin mixture into about 20 golf ball–sized balls. Gently dust each croquette with the flour, shaking off any excess. Coat with the egg, then with the *panko,* lightly pressing the *panko* in place with your fingertips, and place on the prepared plate. (At this point, the croquettes can be frozen by arranging them in a single layer on a platter or rimmed baking sheet in the freezer; when frozen, transfer to a zippered plastic bag, seal, and store frozen for up to 3 months. Deep-fry them directly from the freezer, keeping the oil temperature 325°–350°F and lowering the temperature if the coating browns too quickly.)

I stack them in a pyramid for an eye-catching presentation as an appetizer. For a main course, serve with shredded green cabbage or a green salad and bowls of rice and *Miso Shiru* (page 28).

6 In a wok or deep, wide saucepan, pour 3 inches of oil and heat to 350°F on a deep-frying thermometer or until a bit of *panko* dropped into the hot oil rises immediately to the surface. Working in batches to avoid crowding, drop the croquettes into the oil one at a time and fry until medium brown and crispy, about 4 minutes. Using tongs or chopsticks, transfer the croquettes to a wire rack or paper towels to drain.

7 Serve the croquettes hot. Pass the *tonkatsu* sauce at the table for drizzling or dipping. Store leftovers airtight in the refrigerator and eat at room temperature the next day.

note: Sometimes *kabocha* pumpkins can have very hard tan-brown calcified "warts" on the green skin. Slice off these tan-brown bits before cooking as they will not soften.

VARIATION If you like, add ground meat or poultry to the croquettes: Heat 1 tablespoon canola or other neutral oil in a small frying pan over medium heat. Add ¼ pound ground beef, pork, or chicken. Sprinkle with 1 teaspoon sugar and cook, stirring often and breaking up the meat with a wooden spatula or spoon, until no longer pink, 4–5 minutes. Sprinkle with 1 teaspoon soy sauce, mix well, and immediately remove from the heat. Add the cooked meat to the mashed pumpkin along with the onion.

Unbelievably crispy on the outside, and all fluffy, creamy deliciousness on the inside, *korokke* are beloved throughout Japan. Once the Japanese adapted the French croquette, they created endless variations on the theme.

POTATO KOROKKE

Potato Croquettes

4 russet potatoes, about 2 pounds total weight

Salt and freshly ground pepper

1 tablespoon canola or other neutral oil, plus more for deep-frying

½ large yellow onion

½ pound ground beef (optional)

1 cup all-purpose flour

2 large eggs

About 2 cups *panko* (page 161)

Karashi (page 158) for serving

Tonkatsu sauce (page 17) for serving

MAKES 12 CROQUETTES

1 In a large saucepan over high heat, combine the potatoes and 1 tablespoon salt with water to cover by about 2 inches and bring to a boil. Adjust the heat to maintain a gentle boil and cook the potatoes, uncovered, until a skewer or chopstick easily pierces through a potato and the potatoes are very soft, 30–45 minutes.

2 Meanwhile, in a frying pan over medium heat, warm the oil. When the oil is hot, add the onion and cook, stirring often, until translucent, 4–5 minutes. Add the beef, if using, and cook, breaking it up with a wooden spoon, until the meat is no longer pink, about 4 minutes. Add ¼ teaspoon salt and ⅛ teaspoon pepper, mix well, and remove from the heat.

3 Drain the potatoes. Hold the potatoes in a clean, dry kitchen towel and rub gently to peel away the skins. Place the peeled potatoes in a large bowl and mash with a potato masher or the back of a fork until fairly smooth. Add the beef mixture and mix well. Let cool a bit.

4 Spread the flour in a small, shallow bowl. Break the eggs into a second small, shallow bowl and beat with chopsticks or a fork until well blended. Spread about 2 cups *panko* in a third shallow bowl. Spread a little *panko* on a flat plate.

Continued on page 58

Continued from page 57

Featuring everything from this basic potato filling to pumpkin, corn, crabmeat, tofu, and many more, the countless *korokke* shops in Japan attest to croquettes popularity. They are always a star on the dinner table. Make extra and freeze them for later.

5 Dampen your hands and form the potato mixture into 12 tightly packed oval shapes, each about 3 inches long, 2 inches wide, and 1 inch thick. Gently dust each croquette with the flour, shaking off any excess. Coat with the egg, then with the *panko*, lightly pressing the *panko* in place with your fingertips, and place on the prepared plate. (At this point, the croquettes can be frozen by arranging them in a single layer on a platter or rimmed baking sheet in the freezer; when frozen, transfer to a zippered plastic bag, seal, and store frozen for up to 3 months. Deep-fry them directly from the freezer, keeping the oil temperature 325°-350°F and lowering the temperature if the coating browns too quickly.)

6 In a wok or deep, wide saucepan, pour 3 inches of oil and heat to 350°F on a deep-frying thermometer or until a bit of *panko* dropped into the hot oil rises immediately to the surface. Working in batches of 4 croquettes to avoid crowding, drop the croquettes into the oil one at a time and fry until medium brown and crispy, about 8 minutes. Using tongs, transfer to a wire rack or paper towels to drain.

7 Serve the croquettes hot with *karashi* (Chinese hot mustard) alongside. Pass the *tonkatsu* sauce at the table for drizzling or dipping. Store leftovers airtight in the refrigerator and eat at room temperature the next day.

VARIATION *Corn Korokke* (Corn Croquettes): Substitute 1 cup fresh or thawed, well-drained corn kernels for the beef, stirring briefly to combine with the onion, and seasoning as directed with the salt and pepper.

When my father-in-law found out that this was one of my favorite dishes, he made it for me. Everyone was amazed at his cooking skill, since 75-year-old Japanese men are rarely found at a stove! This side dish is often found in a *bento* (boxed lunch), at a picnic, and on the dinner table. When it is cooked just right, it is sweet and savory and has a crumbly, floury, yet moist texture.

OTOOSAN NO KABOCHA NIMONO

My Father-in-Law's Sweet Simmered Pumpkin

1 *kabocha* pumpkin, about 1¾ pounds

1¼ cups dashi (page 156) or chicken or vegetable broth

1½ tablespoons mirin

1 tablespoon sugar

¼ teaspoon salt

¾ teaspoon soy sauce

SERVES 6 TO 8 AS A SIDE DISH

1 Halve and seed the pumpkin. Using a vegetable peeler, remove random strips of the skin so the pumpkin has a mottled appearance, leaving most of the skin intact but allowing the cooking liquid to flavor the pumpkin. Cut the pumpkin into 1½-by-2-inch chunks and place skin down in a deep frying pan.

2 Measure the dashi in a glass measuring pitcher, add the mirin, sugar, salt, and soy sauce, stir well, and pour the mixture into the pan, reaching about halfway up the sides of the pumpkin pieces. Cover with a drop-lid (page 11), bring to a boil over high heat, reduce the heat to medium-low, and simmer until the pumpkin is tender, 20-25 minutes.

3 Remove from the heat, take off the lid, and allow the pumpkin to sit in the cooking liquid for 15-20 minutes so it soaks up most of the liquid. Serve warm or at room temperature.

In this recipe, soft, rich, quickly-fried eggplant is topped with a sweet and gingery ground chicken "gravy"—the same sauce could also be paired with soft tofu. Quickly frying the eggplant in oil gives this dish richness without an oily taste. Using dark purple Japanese eggplants (or their lavender Chinese counterparts) is ideal.

NASU NO SOBORO ANKAKE

Eggplant with Gingery Chicken

FOR THE SAUCE

¾ pound ground chicken

2 tablespoons plus ¾ teaspoon soy sauce

1 teaspoon ginger juice (page 157)

1 teaspoon mirin

1 tablespoon plus ¾ teaspoon sugar

1 tablespoon cornstarch dissolved in 5 teaspoons water

4 Japanese or Chinese eggplants, about 1 pound total weight

Canola or other neutral oil

1 tablespoon soy sauce

1-inch piece fresh ginger, peeled, cut lengthwise into super-thin strips, and soaked in cold water for garnish

SERVES 2

1 To make the sauce, in a saucepan over medium heat, combine the chicken, 1 cup plus 2 tablespoons water, the soy sauce, ginger juice, mirin, and sugar. Cook, stirring often and breaking up the meat with a spatula until the meat resembles bread crumbs, is melded into the sauce, and is no longer pink, about 5 minutes. Stir the cornstarch-water mixture, then pour it slowly into the pan, stirring until the sauce thickens, about 1 minute. Remove from the heat.

2 Trim the eggplants and halve lengthwise. Lightly score the skin with ¼-inch cross-hatching. In a large frying pan over medium-high heat, warm enough oil to crisp the eggplants without deep-frying. When the oil is hot, working in batches if needed, add the eggplants, cut sides down, and cook, without turning, until lightly browned, about 4 minutes. Using tongs, carefully turn the eggplants and cook until soft, about 5 minutes longer. Lower the heat if needed to keep the eggplants from burning. Remove from the heat and sprinkle with the soy sauce.

3 Just before the eggplants are ready, gently reheat the sauce. Divide the eggplants, skin side up, between 2 shallow bowls and spoon the sauce over the top. Drain the ginger to garnish each bowl and serve right away.

VARIATION *Kabocha no Soboro Ankake* (Pumpkin with Gingery Chicken Sauce): Seed ½ *kabocha* pumpkin and cut into 1½-inch unpeeled chunks. Steam over simmering water until tender, 15–20 minutes. Divide the pumpkin between 2 shallow bowls, top with the sauce, and serve.

Traditionally, *dengaku* is firm tofu threaded onto flat wooden skewers, topped with miso, and grilled. Here, eggplant is topped with a sweet, rich miso sauce and then broiled until the topping is bubbling and delectable.

NASU DENGAKU

Eggplant with Miso Topping

FOR THE MISO TOPPING

5 tablespoons white miso

2½ tablespoons sugar

1 tablespoon mirin

1 large egg yolk

4 Japanese or Chinese eggplants, about 1 pound total weight

1 tablespoon sesame oil

1 tablespoon canola or other neutral oil

Toasted sesame seeds (page 162) for garnish

SERVES 4 AS A SIDE DISH

1 To make the miso topping, in a small saucepan over medium-low heat, stir together the miso, sugar, mirin, egg yolk, and ½ cup water and whisk constantly until the sugar is dissolved and the sauce is very smooth, about 4 minutes. Do not allow it to boil. Remove from the heat and set aside.

2 Trim each eggplant and halve lengthwise. Lightly score the cut sides with ¼-inch cross-hatching to help the miso topping adhere to the eggplant.

3 Preheat the broiler. In a large frying pan over medium-high heat, warm the sesame and canola oils. When the oils are hot, working in batches if needed, add the eggplants, cut sides down, and cook, without turning, until lightly browned, about 4 minutes. Using tongs, carefully turn the eggplants and cook until they are soft but still hold their shape, about 4 minutes longer. Lower the heat if needed to keep the eggplants from burning.

4 Transfer the eggplants, cut side up, to a broiler pan. Spread an equal amount of the miso topping on the eggplants. Broil about 4 inches from the heat source until the miso topping just begins to brown, about 5 minutes. Remove from the broiler and garnish with the sesame seeds. Serve piping hot.

This addictive dish is a very popular *otsumami* (appetizer), and my sister-in-law Emiko is the creator of this version. If you have trouble locating chili bean paste, you can use any Asian chili paste that you like. If you can find only American or Italian globe eggplants, you can still make the recipe.

NASU NO AGEBITASHI

Spicy Sweet-&-Sour Eggplant

FOR THE SAUCE

1 teaspoon minced garlic

1 tablespoon peeled and minced fresh ginger

¼ cup mirin

¼ cup soy sauce

¼ cup rice vinegar

1 teaspoon chili bean paste

About 1 tablespoon sugar

Canola or other neutral oil for deep-frying

8 Japanese or Chinese eggplants, about 2 pounds total weight, trimmed and cut crosswise into 2-inch-thick rounds

3 tablespoons minced green onion, including tender green tops, for garnish

SERVES 4

1 To make the sauce, in a small saucepan over low heat, stir together the garlic, ginger, mirin, soy sauce, vinegar, bean paste, and sugar. (I prefer a small amount of sugar, but add more if you like more sweetness.) Cook, stirring constantly, until the sugar dissolves, about 2 minutes. Remove from the heat and set aside.

2 In a wok or deep, wide saucepan, pour 3 inches of oil and heat to 350°F on a deep-frying thermometer or until bubbles immediately form around a wooden chopstick held upright in the pan. Working in batches to avoid crowding, add the eggplant rounds. Fry, turning as needed, until soft and lightly browned, 4-5 minutes. Using chopsticks or tongs, transfer to a wire rack or paper towels to drain.

3 Pour the sauce into a serving bowl, add the eggplant rounds, and stir lightly to coat. Garnish with the green onions and serve warm or at room temperature.

Lightly cooked spinach with a sweet, nutty dressing is one of the most popular vegetable dishes to make its way from Japan to the rest of the world. You'll want to eat this dressing on everything: I like it on green beans cooked tender-crisp and still bright green, cold shredded chicken, steamed broccoli, or shelled edamame. Kids will eat any vegetable with this sauce.

HORENSO NO GOMA-AE

Spinach in Sesame Dressing

FOR THE DRESSING

¼ cup toasted sesame seeds (page 162), plus more for garnish

1½ tablespoons sugar

1½ tablespoons soy sauce

1½ teaspoons sake

1 large bunch spinach

SERVES 2

1 To make the dressing, using a *suribachi* (mortar and pestle, see page 12), grind the sesame seeds into a rough powder. Add the sugar and grind briefly to combine. Transfer to a bowl, reserving a teaspoon of the sesame-sugar powder for garnish. Add the soy sauce and sake and stir until well blended.

2 Clean the spinach thoroughly in several changes of water, drain, and dry. Place on paper towels with the root ends together.

3 Have ready a large bowl of ice water. Bring a large pot of water to a boil and add the spinach, root ends first, submerging the leaves in the water. Cook for 30 seconds and, using tongs or chopsticks, quickly transfer the spinach to the ice water to stop the cooking and preserve the bright green color, keeping the root ends together. Using your hands, squeeze any excess water from the spinach, transfer to a cutting board, trim and discard the root ends, and chop the leaves into small pieces.

4 Place the spinach in a large bowl. Drizzle with some dressing and toss. Add enough dressing so the spinach is generously coated but not wet and toss until well combined. Serve in individual bowls and garnish with toasted sesame seeds and the reserved sesame-sugar powder.

I was surprised when potato salad showed up first in a *bento* (lunch box) I bought for lunch every day from the corner store, and then on my mother-in-law's dinner table. Finally, something I recognized! Japanese-style potato salad is a widely popular "adopted" side dish.

OKAASAN NO POTATO SARADA

My Mother-in-Law's Potato Salad

Salt

4 russet potatoes, about 2 pounds total weight

½ large English cucumber

½ large carrot, peeled, halved lengthwise, and cut into ¼-inch-thick half-moons

1 tablespoon fresh lemon juice

½ Granny Smith or other tart apple

½ yellow onion, quartered and sliced paper thin

3 slices smoked or boiled ham, cut into small pieces

About ½ cup mayonnaise

Freshly ground pepper

Cherry tomatoes or strawberries, stems removed and halved through the stem end, for garnish

SERVES 8 AS A SIDE DISH

1 In a large saucepan over high heat, combine 1 tablespoon salt and the potatoes with water to cover by about 2 inches and bring to a boil. Adjust the heat to maintain a gentle boil and cook the potatoes, uncovered, until a skewer or chopstick easily pierces through a potato and the potatoes are very soft, 30–45 minutes.

2 Halve the cucumber lengthwise and seed (if any). Slice crosswise into ¼-inch-thick half-moons, place in a colander set over a large bowl, sprinkle with ¼ teaspoon salt, and let stand for 30 minutes. Rinse the salt off of the cucumber slices. Using your hands, squeeze them several times to extract as much water as possible. Pat the cucumber dry with paper towels.

3 Drain the potatoes. Hold the potatoes in a clean, dry kitchen towel and rub gently to peel away the skins. Place the peeled potatoes in a bowl, add 1 teaspoon salt, and mash roughly with the back of a fork, leaving some chunks.

4 In a small saucepan, combine the carrot and 1 cup water, bring to a boil, and cook until tender but not mushy, about 4 minutes. Drain and immediately rinse under running cold water to halt the cooking.

The additions of cucumber, apple, and ham are typical of the universally accepted Japanese version of this Western classic. This salad is a great side dish to *Hamburg* (page 142), *Tonkatsu* (page 110), and *Ebi Furai* (page 102), and at a Western-style summer barbecue.

5 Fill a bowl with water. Add the lemon juice. Peel and core the apple half. Cut lengthwise into ½-inch-thick slices and immediately immerse them in lemon water to prevent darkening.

6 In a large bowl, combine the carrot, onion, cucumber, and ham. Drain the apple and add to the bowl with ½ cup mayonnaise and mix well. Add the potatoes and mix until just combined (do not overmix; the potato texture should be between roughly mashed and a little chunky). Taste and adjust the seasoning with salt and pepper. Add more mayonnaise if the salad seems dry.

7 Garnish with the cherry tomatoes (or strawberries), arranging them around the edge, and serve at room temperature.

✿ **VARIATION** *Makaroni Sarada* (Macaroni Salad): Substitute 2 cups cooked elbow macaroni for the potatoes and cut the cucumber, carrot, apple, and onion into smaller pieces to match the size of the macaroni.

Rice & Noodles

Rice is the most important food in the Japanese diet, and in Japan you see rice paddies nearly everywhere—even across the street from the supermarket in Shohei's hometown! Children are weaned on thin rice gruel, and a bowl of rice accompanies nearly every meal. *Donburi*, a bowl of hot rice topped with meat, fish, or vegetables, came about from the old tradition of pouring leftover soup over rice to make a meal and has evolved into a wildly popular one-dish meal. Rice is so central to the Japanese table that I usually keep some warm rice in the rice cooker or cook extra batches and freeze it so I can always put together a meal quickly.

Noodles are a favorite, too, as the growing popularity of ramen in the West attests. Japanese cooks have access to many, many different varieties of noodles, but in the United States, the choices are limited, so I have restricted the recipes in this chapter to the widely available ramen, soba, and udon.

Noodles are eaten for lunch, as an afternoon or late-night snack, or for dinner. In Japan, the range of presentations is dramatic. Office workers eat noodles *tachigui* style, at stand-up noodle shops, where you buy a ticket from a vending machine and your hot soba or udon noodle soup, udon topped with curry sauces, or other simple noodle dish is served to you in under three minutes—and consumed just as fast. Or, you can go to an elegant restaurant where the soba is handmade and painstakingly styled on the finest hand-thrown ceramic tableware. At home, noodles are fried or served in a soup, in a *nabemono* (one-pot dish), or as a salad. Italian spaghetti is also popular, but prepared to please a Japanese taste: with spicy codfish roe, quick-boiled squid, soy-based sauces, and a sprinkle of *yakinori*.

No matter what type of noodle you are eating, a strict etiquette is in force whenever you eat a noodle soup: you are encouraged to slurp the noodles, which ensures that you will enjoy them while they are still piping hot (as you slurp, you inhale air, which helps to cool off the noodles and thus avoid a burned mouth). Use caution when you slurp. I have ruined many a nice shirt by splattering my noodles.

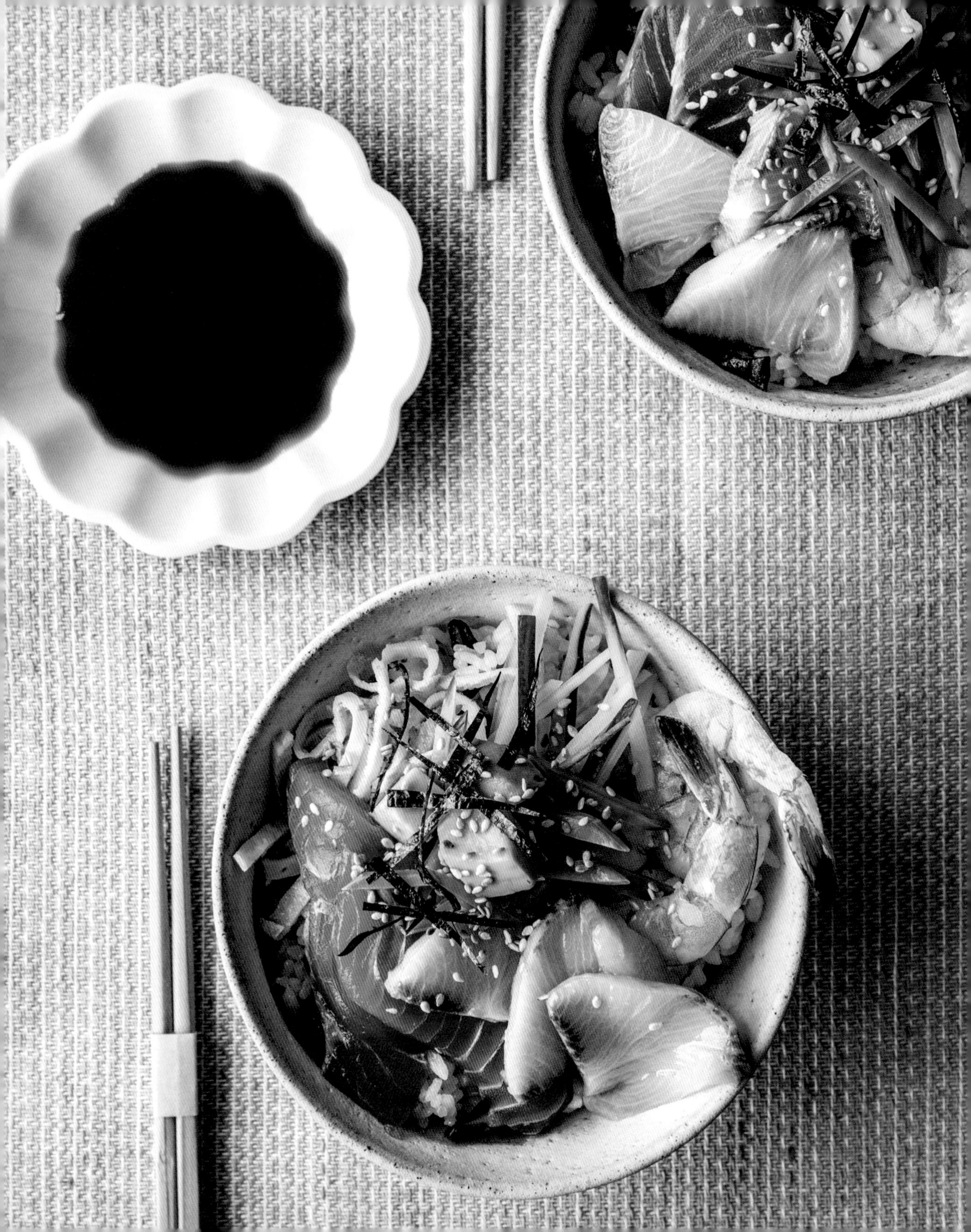

Mastering the art of creating traditional *nigiri sushi* (small pads of rice topped with raw fish) is best left to those who are willing to devote several years to intensive study and apprenticeship. Japanese eat sushi in restaurants or buy it from take-out establishments.

CHIRASHIZUSHI

Home-Style "Sushi" over Rice

FOR THE TOPPINGS

Rice vinegar

2 teaspoons sugar

6 ounces raw shrimp, peeled and deveined; fresh, cooked crabmeat, picked over for shell fragments and cartilage; and/or cooked *surimi* (imitation crabmeat)

Salt

1 small English cucumber

2 ripe avocados

12-20 snow peas, trimmed

2 large eggs

1 tablespoon canola or other neutral oil

2 ounces smoked or fresh, raw sushi-grade salmon, cut into bite-sized strips (optional)

FOR THE MUSHROOMS

2 tablespoons soy sauce

1 teaspoon mirin

1 tablespoon sake

2 tablespoons sugar

6 fresh shiitake mushrooms, stems removed

1 To prepare the toppings, in a bowl, stir together 2 tablespoons rice vinegar and 1 teaspoon of the sugar until the sugar is dissolved. If using shrimp, fill a saucepan with salted water and bring to a boil. Add the shrimp, cook until pink and beginning to curl, about 3 minutes, then drain. When cool enough to handle, slice each in half lengthwise. Add the shrimp to the vinegar mixture and marinate up to 1 hour. If using crabmeat and/or *surimi*, marinate in the vinegar mixture as well.

2 Cut the cucumber in half crosswise, then cut into paper-thin matchsticks 1-2 inches long. Cube the avocados, place in a bowl, and toss with rice vinegar to prevent browning. Have ready a bowl of ice water. Blanch the snow peas in boiling water for 1 minute, drain, immerse in the ice water, drain again, and slice diagonally into bite-sized pieces. Set aside.

3 In a bowl, beat the eggs with a fork or chopsticks until well blended. Add the remaining 1 teaspoon sugar and a pinch of salt and stir until the sugar dissolves. In a 10-inch nonstick frying pan over medium-high heat, warm the oil. When the oil is hot, pour in the egg mixture and swirl to cover the bottom of the pan. Cook, gently lifting the edges to let the uncooked egg flow underneath, until the bottom is set but not browned and the top is relatively dry, 4-5 minutes. Carefully slide the eggs out of the pan onto a flat plate and blot with a paper towel. Let cool, then cut into fine bite-sized shreds called *kinshi tamago* (shredded omelet topping). Set aside.

Continued on page 72

Continued from page 71

Chirashizushi is simply sushi toppings scattered over a bowl of *sushimeshi*. The taste is similar to the sushi you eat in restaurants but is much easier to prepare. The idea is to make the dish both look pretty and taste good. Toppings can vary based on the fresh sushi-grade fish available to you.

FOR THE SUSHI RICE

¼ cup rice vinegar

2 tablespoons sugar

¾ teaspoon salt

3 cups hot cooked rice (see *Gohan*, page 73)

Yakinori (page 159), shredded or torn into small pieces, for garnish

Toasted sesame seeds (page 162) for garnish

Soy sauce for serving

Wasabi for serving (optional)

SERVES 4

4 To prepare the mushrooms, in a small saucepan over medium-low heat, combine 2 cups water, the soy sauce, mirin, sake, and sugar. Bring to a simmer, stirring to dissolve the sugar. Add the mushrooms and cook until the liquid is greatly reduced and the mushrooms are thoroughly flavored but not burned, 15–20 minutes. Remove from the heat and let cool completely in the liquid, then remove from the liquid and thinly slice them. Set aside.

5 Meanwhile, prepare the sushi rice: In a small saucepan over low heat, combine the rice vinegar, sugar, and salt and stir until the sugar and salt are dissolved. Place the hot cooked rice in a large shallow bowl, spreading it evenly. Sprinkle the warm vinegar mixture evenly over the hot rice and, using a wooden rice spatula or wooden spoon, mix in the vinegar, repeatedly cutting down into the rice, turning it over to season it evenly, and mixing until well combined. Let cool to room temperature.

6 Mix the mushrooms into the cooled rice, distributing them evenly, and divide the rice mixture among 4 bowls. Divide evenly and decoratively arrange the seafood, omelet shreds, salmon (if using), cucumber, avocado, and snow pea toppings on the rice and garnish with *yakinori* and sesame seeds. Serve at room temperature (chilling hardens the rice) with small individual bowls for soy sauce and wasabi (if using) into which to dip the toppings.

toppings variation: Raw sushi-grade tuna or yellowtail; prepared salmon roe *(ikura)* or flying fish roe *(tobiko);* flaked water-packed canned tuna

note: Japanese markets carry bottled seasoned rice vinegar for sushi rice. To use it, substitute ¼ cup of it in place of the vinegar mixture.

Nearly every kitchen in Japan has a rice cooker. They are amazing devices, using fuzzy-logic technology to cook perfect grains every time. Japanese are very particular about their rice—my husband can taste the difference between the excellent California-grown rice we eat and the rice grown in Japan. To cook rice using your rice cooker, follow its instructions and use the measuring cup provided.

GOHAN

Steamed Rice

2 CUPS COOKED RICE
(serves 2)

1 cup short-grain white rice

1¼ cups water

3 CUPS COOKED RICE
(serves 3)

1½ cups short-grain white rice

1¾ cups of water

1 In a heavy saucepan with a tight-fitting lid (see-through, if possible), rinse the rice, massaging it with your hands, pouring off the cloudy water, and adding fresh water until the water is nearly clear. Drain well after the final rinse.

2 Add the measured water to the rice in the pan, cover, and bring to a boil over high heat. When the lid jiggles (remember, no peeking), reduce the heat to low, and cook until the liquid is completely absorbed, about 15 minutes. Remove from the heat, leaving the rice in the covered pan and without lifting the lid (for good rice texture) for 15 minutes longer.

3 With a wooden rice paddle or spoon, fluff the rice, and serve.

🌸 **note:** Washing the rice grains was one of the first tasks my mother-in-law entrusted me with in the kitchen, and as with so many things in Japan, there is a proper way to do it: the rice must be massaged vigorously under running cold water for a good four to five minutes, until the washing water runs clear. The idea is to release the starch, or talcum, that coats the kernels, thus ensuring that the cooked rice will have the correct stickiness and a clean taste.

Before heading into work in Tokyo, I often stopped at a little stand where an elderly woman sold nothing but rice balls. *Onigiri* is a quintessential Japanese food: made by moms for breakfast, lunch boxes, and picnics. It is the ideal handheld food (the nori wrapper keeps the sticky rice from getting all over your hand).

ONIGIRI

Rice Balls with Salmon Filling

1 teaspoon salt

1 cup warm cooked rice
(see *Gohan*, page 73)

4 teaspoons cooked flaked
fresh salmon or flaked
canned salmon

2 sheets *yakinori*
(page 159), halved

SERVES 2

1 In a shallow bowl, dissolve the salt in 1 cup water. Dip your hands into the salted water, then grab ¼ cup of the rice. Using your hands, shape the rice into a small, fat triangle, then use your thumb to create an indentation in the center. Place a teaspoonful of the salmon in the hollow, dampen your hands lightly again, and pat the rice over the hollow to encase the salmon. Repeat to create 3 more rice balls.

2 Dry your hands thoroughly. With the pointed end of the rice triangle facing the ceiling, wrap the nori around the bottom of each triangle, leaving the point showing between the open ends of the nori. Eat right away, or pack in your lunch box for later.

Step-by-step *Onigiri* assembly

🌸 **VARIATION** *Yaki Onigiri* (Grilled Rice Balls): These rice balls have no filling or nori. Instead, once compactly formed, they are brushed with soy or miso and broiled until they are crispy and chewy on the outside and soft on the inside. As they are broiling (or grilling), evenly drizzle both sides of each triangle with 1 teaspoon soy sauce or brush with 1 teaspoon white miso. Broil, turning once, until both sides are very browned. Do not allow them to burn; especially watch the miso, which can burn quickly. These *onigiri* are delicious hot.

🌸 **note:** Experiment with fillings. Try tempura shrimp, chicken salad, codfish roe, Japanese pickles, tunafish with mayo, or cooked and crumbled *tsukune* (page 134).

Popular in homes and at lunch counters, this is one of my husband's specialties. Sometimes he adds sliced Chinese sausage and/or cooked crabmeat to the rice. It is a fantastic way to use up leftovers and is often the centerpiece of a family meal, accompanied by *Gyoza* (page 115), *Kara-age* (page 123), or *Miso Shiru* (page 28). This recipe is for the Kaneko house-special *chahan*.

CHAHAN

Japanese-Style Fried Rice

6 slices thick- or regular-cut bacon, cut into 1-inch pieces

1 tablespoon canola or other neutral oil, plus ½ teaspoon sesame oil

2 large eggs, lightly beaten

½ medium yellow onion, minced

5 green onions, including tender green tops, minced

3 cups cooked rice, preferably day-old rice cold from the refrigerator

1 chicken bouillon cube, crushed to a powder

1 tablespoon oyster sauce

¼ cup frozen peas

¼ cup frozen corn kernels

Salt and freshly ground pepper

SERVES 4

1 In a frying pan over medium-high heat, fry the bacon until fat starts to render but the bacon does not crisp, about 4 minutes. Using a slotted spoon, transfer the bacon to paper towels to drain. Discard the bacon fat.

2 Heat a wok or large frying pan over high heat until smoking. Add the sesame and canola oils and swirl the pan to coat the bottom and sides with the oils. Immediately add the eggs and, using a ladle, stir the eggs around the pan, swirling them until they begin to solidify, about 30 seconds. Add the yellow onion and cook 1 minute longer, continuing to use the ladle to swirl the mixture around the pan. Mix in the green onions. Place all of the rice on top of the egg mixture, using the back of the ladle to press the rice into the egg mixture and to break up lumps in the rice. Cook, continuing to press the lumps out of the rice, until all the lumps are gone and the rice, eggs, and onions are well combined, about 2 minutes. Add the bouillon powder and oyster sauce, pressing them into the rice and mixing well. Add the frozen peas and corn (they will thaw as they cook) and the reserved bacon and mix well. Flip the rice by holding the pan's handle and jerking it toward you repeatedly for about 1 minute or use a large spatula to flip the rice. Season to taste with salt and pepper. Turn out onto a platter or into a large bowl and serve steaming hot.

Nigiri sushi is not a homemade food in Japan. Sushi chefs spend many years learning about the fish, how to make sushi rice, and mastering the techniques for the best piece of *nigiri* (bite-sized piece of fish-topped sushi rice). But some simple types of sushi are made at home. *Hosomaki*—a "thin" roll—is a long roll of sushi rice with various fillings wrapped in a crisp nori sheet.

HOSOMAKI

Simple Rolled Sushi

CALIFORNIA ROLL

4 sheets *yakinori* (page 159)

1 cup sushi rice (page 72)

1 avocado, sliced and sprinkled with a little rice vinegar to prevent browning

6 ounces crab stick or crabmeat, picked over for shells and cartilage

½ English cucumber, seeded and cut into matchsticks

Wasabi paste (optional)

Soy sauce for serving

Pickled sushi ginger for serving

YIELDS 4 ROLLS

1 Lay a piece of plastic wrap on a bamboo sushi rolling mat, a flexible silicone baking sheet, or a clean kitchen towel. Lay one sheet of *yakinori*, shiny side down, on the plastic wrap. Moisten your fingertips with cold water, then grab ¼ cup of the rice, and spread it, using your fingers, in a thin layer on the nori without packing it down. Leave a 1-inch border without rice at the top end of the nori. In the center of the rice layer, place ¼ of the avocado slices in a row across the rice. Right above that, similarly place the cucumber across the rice (enough to lay along the length of the roll), then 1½ ounces of crab sticks or crabmeat. Using your index finger, take a small dab of wasabi, if using, and smear it across the rice just above the crab.

2 To roll, start at the end closest to you and, using both hands, hold the rolling mat and roll once over the filling, pressing down with the roll just above where the fillings stop. Unroll the bamboo mat to lie flat (you will have a partial roll in the center of the mat). Starting again, lift the mat and roll it over the partial roll, encircling it, then roll all the way to the top. Remove the bamboo mat and plastic wrap. Repeat, using the remaining ingredients, to make 3 more rolls.

3 Using a very sharp knife, slice the long roll into 1½-inch rounds. Serve with soy sauce for dipping, a dab of wasabi (if using), and sliced pickled sushi ginger.

🌸 **note:** Sushi roll fillings can range from very traditional to more creative options. Try drained canned tuna mixed with spicy or regular mayonnaise, cooked flaked salmon with or without mayo, slivered smoked salmon or asparagus with cream cheese, or cooked shrimp chopped with green onion.

Continued on page 78

Continued from page 77

1 Spread rice in a thin layer over the nori, leaving a border.

2 Add avocado, cucumber, crabmeat, and dab of wasabi.

3 Start at the end closest to you, using both hands to roll.

4 Roll the mat once over the filling to where the fillings stop.

5 Unroll the bamboo mat to lie flat.

6 Starting again, lift the mat, and roll all the way to the top.

SUSHI Who hasn't heard of sushi? The term embraces a wide range of preparations that typically combine vinegared rice with fresh raw fish, shellfish, or fish roe. Some cooked and preserved items are used as well, such as boiled octopus, sweet egg omelet, vinegared mackerel, and more. Sushi, as I have already noted, is best enjoyed at restaurants or bought from take-out shops that specialize in its preparation, rather than made at home. Here are the basic types you will encounter:

Battera Rice and usually vinegared fish pressed in a mold

Chirashizushi Fish and vegetables over rice

Gunkan An Mounded rice with sea urchin or salmon roe on top, wrapped in nori strip

Hosomaki Long, thin roll of rice filled with fish or vegetables wrapped in nori

Nigiri Mounded rice usually topped with raw fish or shellfish or sweet egg omelet

Temaki Rice and a filling in nori rolled into a cone

Oyako literally means "parent and child"—the chicken and the egg—and this homey dish is a key recipe in every housewife's repertoire. Popular variations include substituting deep-fried chicken or pork cutlet (see *Katsudon*, page 110) or thinly sliced beef for the chicken.

OYAKO DONBURI

Chicken & Egg Rice Bowl

FOR THE SAUCE

1 tablespoon sake

3 tablespoons soy sauce

2 tablespoons mirin

1½ tablespoons sugar

1 cup chicken broth

2 small boneless, skinless chicken thighs, trimmed of visible fat and meat cut into bite-sized pieces

½ yellow onion, thinly sliced

4 large eggs

1½ cups hot cooked rice (see *Gohan*, page 73)

2 green onions, julienned, for garnish (optional)

SERVES 2

1 To make the sauce, in a small frying pan over medium-high heat, combine the sake, soy sauce, mirin, sugar, and broth and bring to a simmer.

2 Add the chicken to the pan and simmer until the chicken is half cooked, about 5 minutes. Add the onion and cook until the chicken is cooked through and the onion is soft, about 5 minutes longer.

3 Meanwhile, break the eggs into a bowl and beat with a fork or chopsticks until well blended. Place about ¾ cup of the rice in 2 wide, shallow bowls.

4 When the chicken is ready, add three-fourths of the beaten egg to the pan, cover, and cook until the egg has just set, 4-5 minutes. Uncover, pour in the rest of the egg, and immediately pour the chicken mixture over the bowls of rice, dividing it evenly. Garnish with green onions, if using, and serve right away with chopsticks and spoons to get every last bit of rice and sauce.

note: In *oyako donburi* (or *oyakodon* for short), the eggs are cooked until just set, which adds to the overall pleasing soft texture of the dish. If you do not like soft-cooked eggs, you can increase the cooking time with the pan covered, but don't let the eggs get hard.

There is nothing more *natsukashii* (nostalgic) than the smell of *yakisoba* cooking at street stands and festivals in Japan. I lived in Tokyo near Yoyogi Park, and almost every weekend in the summer *yakisoba* stands were up and running. Since the ingredients and cooking tools are so simple, it is found just about anywhere.

YAKISOBA

Saucy Panfried Noodles with Pork & Vegetables

6 slices thick-cut bacon

2 tablespoons canola or other neutral oil

½ carrot, peeled and sliced into strips about 2 inches long and ½ inch wide

½ head green cabbage, cut into 1-inch squares

½ yellow onion, sliced into ¼-inch-thick wedges

2 packages (14 ounces each) *yakisoba* noodles

About 2 tablespoons *yakisoba* sauce (page 17) or 1-2 tablespoons Worcestershire sauce

Salt and freshly ground pepper

Aonori (page 161) and *beni shoga* (page 157) for garnish (optional)

SERVES 4

1 Place the bacon in a single layer between 2 layers of paper towels and microwave on high for 3 minutes until cooked through but not crispy, or cook the bacon in a frying pan over medium-high heat, turning as needed, 4-5 minutes. Cut into 2-inch pieces and set aside.

2 Heat a wok or large frying pan over high heat until hot. Add the oil and swirl the pan to coat the bottom and sides with oil. When the oil is hot, add the carrot, cabbage, and onion and stir-fry about 2 minutes. Add the bacon and stir to combine. Add the noodles, stir-fry 1 minute, then add ¼ cup water, cover the pan, and cook 1 minute longer. Uncover and allow any remaining water to evaporate.

3 Add some sauce and continue to stir-fry to combine the sauce with the noodles and vegetables, 1-2 minutes. Season with salt and pepper and transfer to a platter. Garnish with *aonori* and *beni shoga*, if using, and serve right away.

note: The *yakisoba* bottled sauce with the strong flavor of soy and Worcestershire sauce is what gives *yakisoba* its distinctive tang. You can make these panfried noodles with Worcestershire sauce alone if you cannot find the proper prepared sauce.

As soon as the first breath of the warm, humid air typical of Japanese summers begins to stir, restaurants start serving this refreshing cold noodle salad with its tangy sauce. The warm-weather alternative to hot ramen noodle soup, *hiyashi chuka* is a lunchtime favorite for office workers and a quick and cooling dinner for families.

HIYASHI CHUKA

Cold Noodle Salad with Sesame-&-Vinegar Sauce

½ pound fresh ramen noodles

FOR THE TOPPINGS

2 large eggs

½ teaspoon sugar

Pinch of salt

1 tablespoon canola or other neutral oil

¼ pound small or medium shrimp

4 slices ham or prepared *chashu*, about 2 ounces total weight

1 English cucumber

4 green onions

1 Fill a large pot with water and bring to a boil. Add the noodles and cook according to the package directions until al dente. Drain and immediately rinse thoroughly under cold running water until completely cool. Set aside.

2 Meanwhile, prepare the toppings: In a bowl, beat the eggs with a fork or chopsticks until well blended. Add the sugar and salt and stir until the sugar is dissolved. In a 10-inch nonstick frying pan over medium-high heat, warm the oil. When the oil is hot, pour in the egg mixture and swirl to cover the bottom of the pan. Cook, gently lifting the edges to let the uncooked egg flow underneath, until the bottom is cooked but not browned and the top is relatively dry, 4–5 minutes. Carefully slide the eggs out of the pan onto a flat plate and blot with a paper towel. Let cool, cut into fine shreds, and set aside.

3 Fill a saucepan with salted water and bring to a boil. Add the shrimp, cook until pink and beginning to curl, about 3 minutes, and drain. When cool enough to handle, peel and devein. Slice the ham into narrow strips. Cut the cucumber crosswise into 3-inch lengths, then julienne. Mince the green onions, including the tender green tops. Set aside with the shrimp.

Continued on page 86

Continued from page 85

Experiment with the toppings: shredded omelet, julienned cucumber, cold roast pork *(chashu)*, green onions, nori, and sometimes tomato wedges are typical, but any chilled seafood, ham, sliced snow peas, carrots, and radishes are also good additions.

FOR THE SAUCE

¼ cup sugar

½ cup soy sauce

¼ cup rice vinegar

2 tablespoons sesame seeds, toasted and ground (page 162)

1 teaspoon sesame oil

Beni shoga (page 157) for garnish (optional)

Yakinori (page 159), shredded, for garnish

Karashi (page 158) for serving

SERVES 2

4 To make the sauce, in a large bowl, stir together ¾ cup water, the sugar, soy sauce, vinegar, sesame seeds, and sesame oil until the sugar is dissolved.

5 To assemble the salad, divide the noodles between 2 large serving bowls. Pour half of the sauce over each bowl of noodles (there will be a lot of sauce). Top each with half of the omelet shreds, shrimp, ham, cucumber, and green onions, arranging them in a traditional pinwheel. Garnish with *beni shoga* and a little *yakinori* and place a dab of *karashi* alongside each serving to mix into the noodles as desired.

note: Traditionally, yellow wheat noodles, typically labeled *hiyashi chuka* or ramen in Asian markets, are used for this dish, and they can occasionally be found fresh, stocked with the refrigerated tofu in regular supermarkets. If you can find them, use them, boiling them until al dente and then cooling them quickly in ice-cold water.

My husband is from Nagano, the heart of Japan's soba country. His hometown has many *soba-ya* (soba restaurants), and every family member has a favorite. Mine is Kusabue, which serves *kurumi* soba, cold noodles with a sweet dipping sauce enriched with walnut paste.

KURUMI SOBA

Cold Soba Noodles with Sweet Walnut Dipping Sauce

1¼ cups dashi (page 156) or water

2 tablespoons soy sauce

2 tablespoons mirin

1 cup walnuts

Sugar

1 package (14 ounces) dried soba noodles

Wasabi for serving (optional)

4 green onions, including tender green tops, minced

SERVES 2

1 In a small saucepan over medium-low heat, warm the dashi. Add the soy sauce and mirin, stir until dissolved, remove from the heat, and let the *tsuyu* sauce cool.

2 Fill a large saucepan with water and bring to a boil.

3 In a small, dry frying pan over medium-high heat, toast the walnuts, shaking the pan to prevent scorching, until fragrant and the nuts have taken on a little color, about 2 minutes. Remove from the heat and let cool. Place the toasted walnuts in a zippered plastic bag, force out the air, and seal closed. Using a meat pounder or the bottom of a large can, crush the nuts until the size of peas. Transfer the crushed nuts to a *suribachi* (see page 12) or a mortar and grind finely. Add 2 teaspoons sugar and grind the sugar into the walnuts. Taste and add more sugar if desired. Add up to 3 tablespoons of the *tsuyu*, reserving the remaining sauce for serving, and grind or mix until the sugar is incorporated and the mixture is a thick paste. Set aside.

4 Have ready a large bowl of ice water. When the water is at a rolling boil, add the soba and cook according to the package directions until al dente. Drain and immediately transfer them to the ice water. Using your hands, swish the noodles to cool them quickly. When cool, drain well and transfer to a large bowl.

5 To serve, place about 2 tablespoons of the walnut paste in each of 2 dipping bowls, add some of the reserved *tsuyu* and the wasabi (if using), and mix until well combined. Then stir in the green onions. To eat, pick up a biteful of the soba with chopsticks, drop it into the dipping sauce, then pick up and eat the soba directly from the dipping bowl.

Continued on page 88

Continued from page 87

This is a micro-regional dish, essentially unknown outside the area. The sweet and nutty dipping sauce (a mixture of *tsuyu*, walnuts, and sugar) is a perfect counterpoint to the cool soba.

note: Soba noodles, which are made from buckwheat flour and have a firm texture and a slightly nutty flavor, are available in many different varieties in Japan. The most common type, which is a pale brown, is made with buckwheat and wheat flours, but some versions incorporate mountain yam, green tea, or other ingredients into the dough. Most of the soba noodles sold in the United States are made from a mix of buckwheat and wheat flours, and the most important thing to remember when boiling them is not to overcook them. They must never be mushy, especially when used in cold noodle dishes. In Japan, the water in which soba is cooked is thought to be full of vitamins and is thus drunk at the end of the meal, mixed with any leftover dipping sauce.

hot soba variations: To make tempura soba, combine ½ cup soy sauce, ½ cup mirin, and 4 cups dashi or reduced-fat, low-sodium chicken broth in a saucepan to make the *tsuyu* broth and bring just to a boil. Follow the directions for cooking and draining (but not cooling) the soba and then divide between 2 large soup bowls. Ladle in the hot broth and top with *Yasai to Ebi Tempura* (page 49).

To make *Tsukimi* soba, make the *tsuyu* broth as directed and bring just to a boil. Follow the directions for cooking and draining (but not cooling) the soba and then divide between 2 large soup bowls. Ladle in the hot broth. Crack an egg into each bowl. The hot broth will partially cook the eggs (see note page 141). Garnish with green onions.

Ramen is truly a Japanese national obsession, now becoming global. *Ramen-ya*, restaurants specializing in ramen dishes, are found all over, with a wide degree of regional variation. I've used instant ramen noodles here, but if you have access to fresh ramen, use them!

SHOHEI NO BUTANIKU TO GOMA RAMEN

Shohei's Special Pork & Sesame Ramen Noodle Soup

1 teaspoon sesame oil

½ pound ground pork

4 slices prepared Chinese roasted pork (*chashu*; optional)

1 tablespoon chili bean paste

1 teaspoon finely minced garlic

2 packages (3½ ounces each) instant ramen noodles

4 cups chicken broth

¼ cup sesame seeds, toasted and ground (page 162), plus more for garnish

Hot chili oil (optional)

2 green onions, including tender green tops, minced

4 slices bamboo shoots (optional)

¼ cup bean sprouts, both ends trimmed (optional)

1 medium-boiled egg, boiled about 7 minutes, peeled and halved lengthwise (optional)

SERVES 2

1 In a frying pan over medium-high heat, warm the sesame oil. When the oil is hot, add the pork, breaking it up with a wooden spatula or spoon. Add the chili bean paste and the garlic and cook, stirring often, until the pork is cooked through and a little crispy, about 4 minutes. Remove from the heat and set aside.

2 Discard the flavor packets from the ramen packages, fill a saucepan with water, and cook the ramen as directed on the package. Meanwhile, in another saucepan, bring the broth to a boil.

3 Just before the noodles are done, divide the ground sesame seeds between 2 large soup bowls and pour in the hot broth, dividing it evenly. Drain the noodles, add half of them to each soup bowl, and swirl them so that they don't stick together.

4 Drizzle in a little hot chili oil, if using, and then top each bowl with half of the pork mixture, *chashu* slices, green onions, bamboo slices, and bean sprouts and a boiled egg half (if using). Garnish with sesame seeds and serve right away.

🍀 **note:** Because ramen broth can be so complex, it is rarely made at home in Japan except with the use of a prepackaged soup base. So when ramen is cooked at home, it is as individualized as the person preparing it.

A specialty from Hokkaido, the cold-weather, northernmost Japanese island, this filling, hearty, ramen from Sapporo is easy to re-create at home. The broth is distinguished by umami-rich miso and a pat of butter added just before serving.

MISO CORN BATA RAMEN

Miso-Flavored Ramen Noodle Soup with Corn & Butter

2 packages (3½ ounces each) instant ramen noodles

4 cups chicken broth

About 2 tablespoons white miso paste

½ cup thawed frozen corn kernels or drained canned corn

2 green onions, including tender green tops, minced

4 slices bamboo shoots (optional)

¼ cup bean sprouts, both ends trimmed (optional)

1 medium-boiled egg, boiled about 7 minutes, peeled and halved lengthwise (optional)

Unsalted butter for serving

SERVES 2

1 Discard the flavor packets from the ramen packages, fill a saucepan with water, and cook the ramen in boiling water as directed on the package.

2 Meanwhile, in another saucepan, bring the chicken broth to a simmer. Scoop out a few spoonfuls of the hot broth into a small bowl, stir in 2 tablespoons white miso until well blended, and slowly incorporate the diluted miso back into the broth, without letting the broth boil. Taste and add more diluted miso, if desired.

3 Drain the noodles, divide them between 2 large soup bowls, and pour in the broth, dividing it evenly. Top each bowl with half of the corn, green onions, bamboo shoots (if using), and bean sprouts (if using) and a boiled egg half (if using). Finish each bowl with unsalted butter and serve right away.

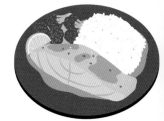

KEWPIE

Fish & Shellfish

In my little neighborhood in Tokyo, there were two major places to buy fish: the big supermarket, which boasted a huge assortment of beautiful fish and shellfish packaged neatly in cellophane, and the local *sakana-ya*, or fish shop, in this case a small storefront run by a fishmonger and his wife and with opening hours that I could never quite figure out. The *sakana-ya* carried a smaller selection of perfect fish, shellfish, and other items from the sea, presented in their natural state—shiny scales, bright eyes, fins and tails intact. I always headed to the fish shop in hopes that it would be open. The fishmonger would walk me through what was good that day, and tell me how to prepare it. He introduced me to things from the sea that I had never seen or heard of, let alone eaten before, and gave me tastes of the *sashimi* (the freshest raw fish) so that I could learn what I liked—and what I didn't. Sometimes I didn't like a particular flavor or texture, but for the most part, the unusual items were both revelatory and wonderful.

Because Japan is an island nation, seafood has always been a focus of the diet, and much of what is eaten is simply grilled or simmered in a light sauce of soy and mirin. When I lived there, I could cook fish or shellfish every day for a year and still not have tried everything. Since the same variety and quality are not available outside of Japan, I have included only the recipes that I have found are possible to re-create authentically in my kitchen in the United States.

Teriyaki is a misunderstood dish in the West. Order it in Japan and you will receive a piece of grilled or panfried fish enhanced with—not overpowered by—a balanced sweet-and-salty glaze of soy sauce, mirin, and sake. The glaze clings to the fish, rather than swamps it, flavoring it perfectly. The same sauce can be used to create yellowtail teriyaki, chicken teriyaki, or beef teriyaki.

SAKE NO TERIYAKI

Salmon Teriyaki

FOR THE MARINADE

¼ cup soy sauce

1 tablespoon sugar

1 tablespoon mirin

1½ teaspoons sake

4 skin-on salmon fillets, each about 6 ounces and 5-6 inches long and ¾ inch thick

1 tablespoon canola or other neutral oil

SERVES 4

1 To make the marinade, in a small bowl, stir together the soy sauce, sugar, mirin, and sake until the sugar is dissolved.

2 Rub your fingers over the fish fillets to check for pin bones, removing them with needle-nose pliers or by pulling them with your fingertips. Pat the fillets dry with paper towels and arrange in a single layer in a shallow dish. Pour the marinade over the fillets, turning them to coat evenly. Cover and marinate in the refrigerator for 30-40 minutes.

3 In a large frying pan over medium heat, warm the oil. When the oil is hot, remove the fillets from the marinade, reserving the marinade, and add to the pan. Cook until medium brown on the first side, about 3 minutes. Carefully turn the fillets and cook the second side until light brown, about 2 minutes longer, watching that the glaze clinging to the fillets does not burn and reducing the heat to medium-low if needed. Pour the reserved marinade over the fish, gently shaking the pan initially to distribute the sauce evenly over the fish, and cook until the sauce is reduced to a syrup and the fish is dark brown, 1-2 minutes longer.

4 Transfer the fish fillets and sauce to individual plates and serve hot.

Shohei and I have been very lucky to have some wonderful Japanese babysitters for our two daughters, Nami and Aya. This recipe from Mizuki-san is assembled and cooked in less than a half hour. Only a little mayonnaise is used, yet it really dresses up the fish. Serve the salmon with *Miso Shiru* (page 28), steamed broccoli and rice, or a side dish of *Sunomono* (page 44).

SAKE TO MAYONNAISU

Broiled Salmon with Mayonnaise

4 salmon fillets, preferably skin on, each about 6 ounces and ¾ inch thick

Salt

Unsalted butter for greasing

4 tablespoons Japanese mayonnaise, preferably Kewpie brand, or regular mayonnaise mixed with 1 teaspoon fresh lemon juice or ½ teaspoon rice vinegar

SERVES 4

1 Rub your fingers over the fish fillets to check for pin bones, removing any you find with needle-nose pliers or by pulling them with your fingertips. Pat the salmon fillets dry with paper towels and salt generously on both sides. Arrange in a single layer in a shallow dish, cover, and refrigerate for at least 10 minutes or up to 1 hour, allowing the salt to "cook" the outer layer and the saltiness to penetrate better than sprinkling with salt and cooking immediately.

2 When you are ready to cook, preheat the broiler with a rack set about 4 inches from the heat source. Lightly butter a rimmed baking sheet and place the fillets, skin side down, on the baking sheet. Broil until lightly browned and bubbly, 6–8 minutes. Carefully turn the fillets (they have a tendency to stick and break) and broil on the second side until the skin is browned and crisp, about 4 minutes longer.

3 Remove the baking sheet from the broiler and top each fillet with 1 tablespoon of the mayonnaise, spreading it evenly or, if the mayonnaise is in a squeeze bottle, squeeze on top in attractive squiggles. Return the salmon to the broiler and broil until the mayonnaise is browned, about 2 minutes longer.

4 Transfer the fillets to individual plates and serve hot.

On most days, my mother-in-law heads to the fish market and buys whatever fish looks good that day—and something always does. Here at home, fresh salmon is one of the most reliable fish you can buy. Happily, it lends itself very well to this recipe, which is also known as *munieru* in Japan — an adaptation of the French style *a la meunière* (dusted with flour and sautéed in butter).

SAKE BATAYAKI

Salmon with Butter & Soy Sauce

4 skin-on salmon fillets, each about 6 ounces and ¾ inch thick

½ teaspoon salt

1 cup all-purpose flour

1½ tablespoons unsalted butter

1 tablespoon canola or other neutral oil

2 teaspoons soy sauce

SERVES 4

1 Rub your fingers over the fish fillets to check for pin bones, removing any you find with needle-nose pliers or by pulling them with your fingertips. Pat the fish fillets dry with paper towels and sprinkle on both sides with the salt. Pour the flour in a shallow bowl or on a piece of aluminum foil and spread into a shallow layer.

2 Heat a frying pan large enough to fit all 4 fillets over medium heat or work in batches. One at a time, and just before cooking, place a salmon fillet on top of the flour and lightly and evenly dust both sides, gently shaking off any excess. Transfer the dusted fillets in batches to a plate. When the pan is hot, add the butter and oil, dividing it as needed. When the butter foams, add the salmon fillets, skin side down, and cook until browned with crisped skin on the first side, 2–3 minutes. Carefully turn the fillets and cook on the second side until browned, with an opaque center when tested with a small knife, 2–3 minutes longer.

3 Just before removing the fillets from the pan, drizzle them with the soy sauce and gently shake the pan to distribute evenly. Transfer the fillets to individual plates and serve hot.

If you have access to fresh clams, this is a quintessential Japanese dish. The most difficult part of this recipe is removing the sand from the clams. This dish is served in homes and turns up on *izakaya* (page 22) menus. The broth should be drunk after the clams have been eaten, which is why you want to make sure it is sand-free.

ASARI NO SAKAMUSHI

Steamed Clams in Sake & Butter Broth

1 pound small, live hard-shelled clams such as Manila or small littleneck

Salt

2 tablespoons unsalted butter

2 cloves garlic, finely minced

2 cups sake

½ bunch fresh chives, thinly sliced, for garnish

SERVES 2

1 Wash the clams under running cold water. Fill a large, wide, deep bowl half full with cold water, add 1 tablespoon salt, and stir until dissolved. Submerge the clams in the bowl and let stand for 1–2 hours (the amount of time for the clams to purge their sand depends on the clam type and where the clams were purchased). Change the soaking water frequently, adding more salt each time, and check if there is sand in the bottom of the bowl. When the bowl is free of sand, drain the clams, rinse thoroughly in fresh water, and drain again. Discard clams that do not close when touched.

2 In a Dutch oven or other large, heavy pot over medium heat, melt 1 tablespoon of the butter. When the butter stops foaming, add the garlic and drained clams. Immediately add the sake, cover, and cook, without lifting the lid, until all the clams have opened, and checking after about 5 minutes. Uncover and discard clams that failed to open. Add the remaining 1 tablespoon butter and stir to mix. Ladle the clams and their broth into bowls, garnish with chives, and serve hot.

Cooked in the same style as *Tonkatsu* (page 110), this is the best fried shrimp you'll ever eat. The light *panko* coating produces incredible crispiness with no grease, and the shrimp fry quickly so it is not a time-intensive meal. I buy more shrimp than I need, bread the extra, and then freeze them for a quick dinner on another day. •

EBI FURAI

Crispy Panko-Fried Shrimp

12 extra-large shrimp, peeled and deveined

½ cup all-purpose flour

1 large egg

About 2 cups *panko* (page 161)

Canola or other neutral oil for deep-frying

Prepared tartar sauce, or ¼ cup mayonnaise mixed with 2 tablespoons tomato ketchup or pickle relish to taste, or *tonkatsu* sauce (page 17) for serving

SERVES 4

1 To keep the shrimp from curling during frying, make 3–4 shallow horizontal cuts across the belly of each shrimp, then stretch it lightly without breaking it until it is straight. Spread the flour in a small, shallow bowl. Break the egg into a second shallow bowl and beat with a fork or chopsticks until well blended. Spread about 1 cup *panko* in a third shallow bowl and spread a little *panko* on a flat plate.

2 One at a time, lightly dust each shrimp with flour, coating evenly and shaking off any excess, dip in the egg, then roll in the *panko*. Using your fingertips, lightly press the *panko* in place and place the shrimp on the prepared plate. Add more *panko* to the bowl as needed.

3 In a wok or deep, wide saucepan, pour 3 inches of oil and heat to 350°F on a deep-frying thermometer or until a bit of *panko* dropped into the hot oil rises immediately to the surface. Working in batches to avoid crowding, drop the shrimp one at a time into the oil and fry until medium to dark brown, about 3 minutes. Using chopsticks or tongs, transfer the shrimp to a wire rack or paper towels to drain.

4 Spoon the tartar sauce into a small bowl and serve the shrimp right away, passing the sauce at the table.

🌸 **VARIATION** *Kaki Furai* (Crispy Fried Oysters): Substitute 20 medium or large jarred oysters for the shrimp. Drain well, then bread and deep-fry as directed. Serve with shredded green cabbage and tomato wedges drizzled with salad dressing and tartar sauce and/or *tonkatsu* sauce and lemon wedges alongside.

With a crispy outside and an interior of molten white sauce laced with crabmeat, this is an indulgent and spectacular version of the *korokke* recipes (page 54) in the Vegetables chapter.

KANI KURIMU KOROKKE

Creamy Crab Croquettes

1 tablespoon unsalted butter

½ yellow onion, minced

¾ cup fresh or canned crabmeat, picked over for shell fragments and cartilage

1 tablespoon white wine

FOR THE WHITE SAUCE

3 tablespoons unsalted butter

¼ cup all-purpose flour

1½ cups whole milk

Pinch of salt

About 1 cup all-purpose flour

1 large egg

About 2 cups *panko* (page 161)

Canola or other neutral oil for deep-frying

Lemon wedges or ½ cup tomato ketchup diluted with ¼ cup hot water for serving

SERVES 4

1 In a small frying pan over medium-high heat, melt the butter. When the butter foams, add the onion and cook, stirring often, until translucent, 2-3 minutes. Add the crabmeat, stir, and add the wine. Cook for about 1 minute to evaporate any liquid, remove from the heat, and set aside.

2 To make the white sauce, in a saucepan over medium heat, melt the butter. When the butter foams, add the flour one tablespoonful at a time and stir constantly to create a smooth paste, about 3 minutes. Do not allow it to color. Slowly add the milk, stirring constantly to prevent lumps. Cook, stirring constantly, until the mixture is thick, glossy, and the consistency of mayonnaise, about 10 minutes. Add the salt, stir well, then add the crab mixture and stir just until combined.

3 Spread the crab mixture in a 1-inch layer in a cake pan and let cool completely. Cover the pan with plastic wrap and refrigerate for at least 2-3 hours or up to overnight so it solidifies and is easier to handle.

4 Spread ½ cup flour in a small, shallow bowl, refilling the bowl as needed. Break the egg into a second shallow bowl and beat with chopsticks or a fork until well blended. Spread about 1 cup of the *panko* in a third shallow bowl, refilling the bowl as needed. Spread a little *panko* on a flat plate.

Although a little time-consuming, believe me, this recipe is well worth the effort. While you're at it, make extra and freeze them to fry for another day. These are a real showstopper.

5 Remove the crab mixture from the refrigerator just before cooking. Using a metal spatula, divide the mixture into 8 equal portions. One at a time, using your hands and working quickly (the heat of your hands softens the mixture, so the less you touch it, the better), form each portion into a small rectangle or cylinder, about 3 inches long and 2 inches wide, and gently dust each croquette with the flour, shaking off any excess. Coat with the egg and then with the *panko*, lightly pressing the *panko* in place with your fingertips, and place it on the prepared plate.

6 In a wok or deep, wide saucepan, pour 3 inches of oil and heat to 350°F on a deep-frying thermometer or until a bit of *panko* dropped into the hot oil rises immediately to the surface. Working in batches of 4 croquettes to avoid crowding, carefully drop the croquettes into the oil one at a time and fry until golden brown, 6-7 minutes. Using a slotted spoon or spatula, carefully remove the croquettes so they don't break open and transfer to a wire rack or paper towels to drain.

7 Serve the croquettes hot with lemon wedges or with the ketchup mixture.

VARIATION *Corn Kurimu Korokke* (Creamy Corn Croquettes): Substitute ¾ cup fresh or thawed, well-drained corn kernels for the crabmeat.

My kids will eat nearly anything if ketchup is involved, but even adults with more evolved tastes will find that this seemingly unsophisticated dish has a complex flavor. In Japan, this is both a popular lunch-counter option and home-style main course. Scatter some frozen green peas for taste and color just before serving.

EBI NO CHIRI SO-SU

Shrimp in Mild Tomato Chili Sauce

¾ pound shrimp, peeled and deveined

1 tablespoon cornstarch

1 tablespoon dry sherry

1 large egg white

3 tablespoons tomato ketchup

½ teaspoon soy sauce

1½ teaspoons sake

1 teaspoon sugar

2 cups canola or other neutral oil

¼ yellow onion, minced

½ teaspoon minced garlic

2 tablespoons peeled and minced fresh ginger

1 teaspoon chili bean paste

2 green onions, including tender green tops, minced, for garnish

2 tablespoons frozen peas (optional) for garnish

SERVES 4

1 In a small bowl, combine the shrimp, cornstarch, sherry, and egg white and stir to evenly coat the shrimp. Let stand at room temperature for 15 minutes.

2 Meanwhile, in another small bowl, stir together the ketchup, soy sauce, sake, and sugar until the sugar is dissolved. Set the bowl near the stove.

3 In a wok or large frying pan over high heat, warm the oil. When it is hot, add the shrimp and stir with a wooden spatula until they are a little crispy, 5-6 minutes. Using tongs or a slotted spoon, transfer the shrimp to a bowl.

4 Pour out all but 2 teaspoons of the oil. Set the wok over medium heat and swirl to coat the bottom and sides with the oil. Add the yellow onion and cook for 1 minute. Add the garlic and ginger and stir-fry briefly, just until fragrant. Add the chili bean paste, stir well, and then stir in the ketchup mixture. Return the shrimp to the pan, raise the heat to high, and cook, stirring, until the ingredients are well combined and the shrimp are coated with the sauce, 1-2 minutes longer.

5 Transfer the shrimp to a serving dish, garnish with the green onions and peas (if using), and serve right away.

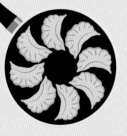

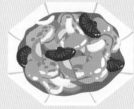

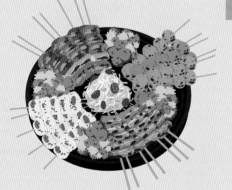

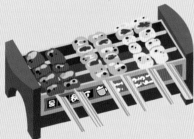

Meat & Poultry

Before I lived in Japan, I thought it was going to be all fish, fish, fish, fish. And, of course, rice. As expected, I did encounter plenty of fish. But to my surprise, when I started eating what regular people eat and began cooking more and more with my mother-in-law and my sister-in-law, I found that they were eating some kind of meat daily, usually chicken or pork but also beef.

Although beef was not part of the Japanese diet until the arrival of the Meiji period in 1868, poultry and pork have a long history on the Japanese table. Japan is a small country, with little grazing land for cattle, so meat has been traditionally thought of as an expensive, hard-to-get ingredient. Now that Japanese tastes have expanded to include some Western dishes, meat and poultry are playing a much larger role in everyday cooking.

Discovering these meat recipes made me think that successfully cooking home-style Japanese dishes was actually possible. The recipes in this chapter might be the ones that surprise you the most, just as they did me. Hamburger, steak, fried chicken—are they really Japanese? Absolutely. If you are nervous at all about cooking and eating Japanese food, you might want to start here.

In Japan, restaurants specializing in *tonkatsu* offer the customer a variety of pork cuts, including *hire* (lean cut), *rosu* (fattier cut), and *kurobuta* ("black pig" from prized Berkshire pigs). A large heap of finely shredded, crisp green cabbage is served alongside the fried pork.

TONKATSU

Crispy Panko-Fried Pork Cutlets

Canola or other neutral oil for deep-frying

2 cups all-purpose flour

1 large egg

About 4 cups *panko* (page 161)

1 teaspoon salt

4 boneless pork loin chops, each about ¼ pound and ½-¾ inch thick (lightly score ¾-inch-thick chops with a sharp knife to ensure even cooking)

Tonkatsu sauce (page 17) for serving

Karashi (page 158; optional) for serving

½ head green cabbage, finely shredded, for serving

Mayonnaise (optional) for serving

Cherry tomatoes, halved, or tomato wedges, for serving

SERVES 4

1 In a wok or deep, wide saucepan, pour 3 inches of oil and heat to 350°F on a deep-frying thermometer or until a bit of *panko* dropped into the hot oil rises immediately to the surface.

2 Meanwhile, spread the flour in a small, shallow bowl. Break the egg into a second bowl and beat with chopsticks or a fork until well blended. Spread 3 cups of the *panko* in a third shallow bowl. Sprinkle a little *panko* on a flat plate.

3 Lightly salt both sides of 1 cutlet, dust with flour, shaking off any excess, and coat with the egg and then with the *panko*. Using your fingertips, lightly press the *panko* in place and set the cutlet on the prepared plate. Repeat with the remaining cutlets, adding more *panko* to the bowl as needed.

4 When the oil is ready, add 1 or 2 cutlets to avoid crowding and fry, turning often, until very crispy and medium brown, about 6 minutes. Using tongs, transfer to a wire rack or paper towels to drain. Repeat with remaining cutlets.

5 Cut the cutlets crosswise into narrow strips, reassemble on individual plates, and drizzle with *tonkatsu* sauce. Add a dab of *karashi* (if using) on the side. Serve the cabbage with *tonkatsu* sauce and a little mayonnaise, if desired, and tomatoes alongside.

VARIATION *Katsudon* (Pork Cutlet and Egg over Rice): Fry 2 cutlets as directed and cut into bite-sized strips. In a frying pan, simmer 1 tablespoon sake, 3 tablespoons soy sauce, 2 tablespoons mirin, 1½ tablespoons sugar, and 1 cup chicken broth. Add ½ cup thinly sliced yellow onion and cook until soft, about 5 minutes. Add 2 beaten eggs, cover, and cook until just set. Add pork and 2 more beaten eggs, cover, and cook about 1 minute. Divide between 2 bowls of rice.

This is a great example of *okaasan no ryori*—"mother's cooking"—and every mother has her own version. Shohei's mother uses a little fatty pork, known as *baraniku*, literally "belly meat," in hers. For vegetarians, omit the bacon and replace the dashi with vegetable broth.

KANEKO NO UCHI NO KENCHIN JIRU

Vegetable Soup with Pork

6 slices thin-cut bacon, cut into 2-inch pieces

2 small russet potatoes

6-inch piece daikon, about 3 inches in diameter, or 10 red radishes, trimmed

1 carrot

1 parsnip

1 tablespoon canola or other neutral oil

5-6 fresh shiitake mushrooms, stems removed and caps sliced ¼ inch thick

1 tablespoon dashi powder or granules (page 156) or chicken bouillon powder, or 1 bouillon cube

About ¼ cup soy sauce

2½ tablespoons mirin

1 tablespoon sugar

½ block any style tofu, about 7 ounces

2 tablespoons minced green onion, for garnish

Ichimi togarashi or *shichimi togarashi* (page 162), for garnish

SERVES 2

1 In a frying pan over medium-high heat, fry the bacon until the fat starts to render but the bacon does not crisp, about 4 minutes. Using a slotted spoon, transfer the bacon to a stockpot. Discard the fat.

2 Peel the potatoes, daikon, carrot, and parsnip. Cut the potato into 1-inch chunks. Lengthwise halve the daikon, carrot, and parsnip, then cut crosswise into ¼-inch-thick half-moons (or cut radishes into ¼-inch-thick slices, if using).

3 Add the oil to the pot over medium-high heat. When the oil is hot, add the potatoes, daikon, carrot, parsnip, and mushrooms and cook, stirring often, for about 2 minutes. Add enough water to cover the vegetables, the dashi powder, ¼ cup soy sauce, the mirin, and sugar and stir well. Bring to a rapid simmer and reduce the heat to medium-low. Using your hands, break the tofu into 2-inch chunks and add to the soup. Continue to cook, uncovered, until the vegetables are soft, 30–40 minutes. Cover the pot if the liquid evaporates before the vegetables are cooked through.

4 Season to taste with salt or soy sauce. Ladle into warmed bowls, garnish with green onion and *ichimi togarashi*, and serve piping hot.

The cooking sauce for this dish is the same one I use for making *Mapo Dofu* (page 27). The fried eggplant is crispy and creamy at the same time, and when combined with the rich sauce, the resulting marriage is perfect over a bowl of rice.

MAPO NASU

Spicy Eggplant with Pork

Mapo Dofu **sauce (page 27, step 1)**

6 green onions

3 cloves garlic, minced

1-inch piece fresh ginger, peeled and minced

4 Japanese or Chinese eggplants, about 1 pound total weight

6 tablespoons canola or other neutral oil

½ pound ground pork

Sesame oil (optional)

3 cups hot cooked rice (see *Gohan*, page 73) for serving

SERVES 4

1 Make the sauce.

2 Mince the white parts and tender green tops of 4 green onions. Mince the white parts of the remaining 2 green onions, then halve the tender green tops lengthwise and slice them crosswise into 1-inch-wide pieces. Place the minced green onions, garlic, and ginger in 3 separate bowls. Reserve the sliced green onion tops for garnish.

3 Trim the eggplants, quarter lengthwise, and cut crosswise into ½-inch-thick pieces. Heat a wok or frying pan over medium-high heat and add 4 tablespoons of the canola oil. When the oil is hot, add the eggplant and stir-fry until soft, about 4 minutes. Transfer to a bowl.

4 Wipe the pan clean and reheat over high heat. Add the remaining 2 tablespoons canola oil and swirl the pan to coat the bottom and sides. When the oil is very hot, add the minced green onions and garlic, stir well, and reduce the heat to medium before the garlic scorches. Add the ground pork and, using a spatula, continue to stir constantly, breaking up the pork. When the pork is just cooked, about 2 minutes, add the chili bean paste and pour in the broth mixture. Mix the ingredients with the sauce until well combined. Add the eggplant, stir well, and heat through. Stir the cornstarch-water mixture, then pour it slowly into the pan, stirring until the sauce in the pan thickens, about 1 minute. Drizzle in a little sesame oil, if you like.

5 Spoon into a serving bowl, garnish with the reserved green onion slices, and serve with individual bowls of rice.

When Shohei and I were living in Tokyo, all I ever had to do to get out of cooking dinner was to ask, "How about the *gyoza* place?" Tokyo's back alleys are filled with tiny little restaurants; the *gyoza* place was one of these. I could never find it on my own in the warren of small restaurants and bars under the train tracks.

GYOZA

Panfried Dumplings

FOR THE FILLING

½ pound Napa or green cabbage, cored

¾ pound ground pork

2 green onions, including tender green tops, minced

3 fresh shiitake mushrooms, stems removed and caps minced

½ bunch fresh chives, minced

1 teaspoon peeled and grated fresh ginger

1 teaspoon minced garlic

1 tablespoon sesame oil

1 tablespoon sake

1 teaspoon soy sauce

1 To make the filling, shred and finely chop the cabbage, then squeeze between paper towels to remove any excess moisture. In a large bowl, combine the cabbage, pork, green onions, mushrooms, chives, ginger, garlic, sesame oil, sake, and soy sauce. Using your hands, mix together just until well combined, avoiding handling the filling too much.

2 Have ready a bowl of water. Place a sheet of waxed paper and the stack of wrappers on a work surface, covering the wrappers with a clean, damp kitchen towel or paper towel to prevent them from drying out. Holding one wrapper in the palm of one hand, place about 1 teaspoon of the filling in the center of the wrapper. With a fingertip, swipe half of the edge of the wrapper with a little water, and then fold the other edge over the filling to meet the dampened edge and pinch the edges together to seal securely. With your fingers, make 4–5 evenly spaced pleats along the sealed edge and place the dumpling, flat side down opposite the pleats, on the waxed paper. Repeat with the remaining filling. At this point, the *gyoza* can be frozen: arrange on a rimmed baking sheet, freeze until solid, transfer to a zippered plastic bag, seal, and freeze for up to 1 month, cooking them directly from the freezer for a few extra minutes when the pan is covered.

Continued on page 116

Continued from page 115

There is nothing better than a *gyoza* with a crispy bottom and a juicy filling and, if you like, beer. These tasty dumplings and beer are natural mates. The dumplings are not difficult to make, but they are time-consuming to stuff and shape, so I recommend you make a whole lot (it is a great group activity!) and freeze them for a quick meal or appetizer.

1 Place 1 teaspoon of the filling in the center of the wrapper.

2 Fold wrapper in half and pinch the edges together to seal.

3 Make 4-5 evenly spaced pleats with your fingers.

4 Place the dumpling flat side down on waxed paper.

At least 48 round, thin *gyoza* wrappers or other Asian dumpling wrappers, about 3 inches in diameter

Canola or other neutral oil

Sesame oil

Soy sauce

Rice vinegar

Hot chili oil

MAKES ABOUT 48 DUMPLINGS

3 Heat a frying pan over high heat until the pan is hot. Working in batches, add 1 tablespoon canola oil and 1 tablespoon sesame oil per batch and swirl to coat the bottom of the pan with the oils. When a drop of water flicked into the oil sizzles instantly, neatly arrange about 12 dumplings per batch in the pan, flat sides down and pleated edges up. Cook undisturbed until the bottoms are lightly browned, about 3 minutes. Add 1 tablespoon water per batch, immediately cover the pan, reduce the heat to medium-high, and cook for 5 minutes. Uncover and cook a few minutes longer until the water has evaporated and the *gyoza* are dark brown and a little crusty on the bottom.

4 To serve, slide a spatula under the *gyoza*, being careful not to tear the wrappers, flip them browned-side up, and neatly line them up on a large platter. Repeat with the remaining *gyoza*.

5 Set out individual dipping bowls and the containers of soy sauce, vinegar, and hot chili oil for diners to create a dip to taste.

Juicy, gingery, and a little sweet, this dish comes together very quickly. I first encountered *shogayaki* at my local Tokyo convenience store late one night after work. I asked my mother-in-law for a from-scratch recipe and now it's a dinner staple with salad and rice.

BUTANIKU NO SHOGAYAKI

Panfried Ginger Pork

1 pound boneless pork loin chops, each 2-3 inches wide

FOR THE MARINADE
2 teaspoons ginger juice (page 157)

3 tablespoons sake

1½ tablespoons mirin

4½ tablespoons soy sauce

Sesame oil

Canola or other neutral oil

SERVES 3 OR 4

1 Put the pork loin in the freezer for about 1 hour (this makes it easier to slice the meat very thinly). Cut the pork into about 12 slices, each ⅛ inch thick.

2 To make the marinade, in a bowl, combine the ginger juice, sake, mirin, and soy sauce and stir well. Add the pork, coating each piece with the marinade. Let stand for 5 minutes, then turn to marinate the second side for at least 5 minutes but no longer than 30 minutes or the pork will harden.

3 Heat a large frying pan over medium-high heat. When the pan is hot, working in 2 batches, add 1½ teaspoons sesame oil and 1½ teaspoons canola oil per batch and swirl the pan to coat the bottom and sides with the oils. When the oils are hot, transfer half of the pork slices to the pan in a single layer. Pour half of the marinade over the pork. Cook the pork, gently shaking the pan occasionally to distribute the sauce, until browned on the first side, about 3 minutes. Turn the pork pieces and cook until the second side is browned but the pork is still juicy, about 3 minutes longer. Transfer the pork to a platter and keep warm. Repeat to cook the remaining pork slices. Serve topped with any pan juices.

In the small town where I first lived, I went to a little restaurant that specialized in pork. I couldn't read the menu, so the waitress brought me their most popular dish, *tonjiru*. In Japan, pork belly *(baraniku)* is used for this soup. If you can find burdock root *(gobo)*, peel it and use in place of the parsnip.

BUTA TONJIRU

Hearty Miso Soup with Pork & Vegetables

½ small daikon, or 10 radishes, peeled and quartered

1 parsnip

1 carrot

1 pound boneless country-style pork rib meat

1-inch piece unpeeled ginger, quartered

1 russet potato, peeled and cut into 1½-inch chunks

½ cup miso, preferably red

1 tablespoon mirin

6 fresh shiitake mushrooms, stems removed and caps halved

4 green onions, including tender green tops, cut diagonally into ½-inch pieces

Shichimi togarashi or equal parts black pepper and cayenne or *ichimi* pepper (page 162) for serving

SERVES 6

1 Peel the daikon, parsnip, and carrot and halve lengthwise. Cut each crosswise into ½-inch-thick half-moons. Slice the meat into pieces 2 inches long, 1 inch wide, and ½ inch thick.

2 In a large saucepan over high heat, bring the meat, 2½ quarts water, and the ginger to a boil. Skim any foam that rises to the surface. Cover partially, reduce the heat to medium, and simmer for about 1 hour for a flavorful broth and very tender meat. Remove the ginger and add the daikon, parsnip, and carrot to the broth, cover partially, and simmer for 15 minutes. Add the potato, cover, and simmer for 10 minutes. Put ¼ cup of the miso into a small bowl, add a few spoonfuls of the soup broth, and stir with a fork or chopsticks until well blended. Reduce the heat to low, add the diluted miso to the pan, stir well, cover, and cook for 20 minutes. Do not allow the soup to boil.

3 Put the remaining ¼ cup miso in the small bowl, add the mirin and a few spoonfuls of the soup broth, stir, and add back to the pan, along with the mushrooms. Cover and continue to cook until the vegetables are very tender, about 15 minutes longer. Stir in the green onions and immediately remove from the heat. Ladle into warmed bowls and serve, passing the *shichimi togarashi* at the table.

note: Versatile "country-style" boneless pork ribs are often cut from the loin or shoulder. They have enough marbling to keep the meat moist, and can withstand low, slow cooking.

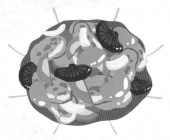

I ate this dish often in the little lunch place near my office in Tokyo, and I always watched the cooks behind the counter make it, hoping to learn the skill necessary to prepare it myself. It has a tangier taste and is not as heavily fried as the Westernized version of the same dish.

SUBUTA

Japanese-Style Sweet-&-Sour Pork

1 carrot

Canola or other neutral oil

1 pound pork tenderloin, cut into 1-inch cubes

2 teaspoons soy sauce

1 teaspoon sake

¼ cup cornstarch

FOR THE SAUCE

¼ cup tomato ketchup

¼ cup sugar

¼ cup rice vinegar

1 teaspoon salt

1 teaspoon sesame oil

1 cup chicken broth

1 tablespoon cornstarch

6 fresh shiitake mushrooms

1 yellow onion

½ large green bell pepper

¼ cup sliced bamboo shoots

3-4 cups hot cooked rice (see *Gohan*, page 73) for serving

SERVES 4

1 Peel the carrot, halve lengthwise, and cut crosswise into ½-inch-thick half-moons. Fill a small saucepan with water and bring to a boil. Add the carrot and blanch for 1 minute. Drain and immediately rinse under running cold water to halt the cooking. Set aside.

2 In a wok or deep, wide saucepan, pour 3 inches of oil and heat to 350°F on a deep-frying thermometer or until bubbles immediately form around a wooden chopstick held upright in the pan.

3 Meanwhile, in a bowl, combine the pork, soy sauce, and sake until the pork is evenly coated. Place the cornstarch in a small, shallow bowl near the stove.

4 When the oil is ready, dust 1 pork cube with the cornstarch, shake off any excess, and drop it into the hot oil. Repeat with the remaining cubes, adding them one at a time and working in batches if needed to avoid crowding. Fry, turning often, until golden brown, about 5 minutes. Using a slotted spoon, transfer to a wire rack or paper towels to drain.

5 To make the sauce, in a bowl, combine the ketchup, sugar, vinegar, salt, sesame oil, and broth, stir well, and place near the stove. In another bowl, stir together the cornstarch and 2 tablespoons water and place near the stove.

I've seen even quicker-cooking versions made with thinly sliced pork coated in cornstarch and sautéed instead of deep-fried. This recipe is a real husband and family hit. Serve with a bowl of rice and some sides. The *Nasu no Agebitashi* (page 63) works well on the side.

6 Remove the stems from the mushrooms and quarter the caps if large or halve the caps if medium-sized. Halve the onion through the stem end and cut into ½-inch-thick slices. Seed the bell pepper, cut lengthwise into 1-inch-wide strips, and halve crosswise.

7 Discard the oil from the pan and return the pan to medium-high heat. When the pan is hot, add 3 tablespoons oil and swirl the pan to coat the bottom and sides. When the oil is hot, add the mushrooms and stir-fry briefly. Add the onion and bell pepper and stir-fry until the onion starts to turn translucent, 3–4 minutes. Add the carrot, bamboo shoots, and fried pork cubes and stir-fry about 1 minute. Pour in the ketchup mixture and mix well to combine all the ingredients with the sauce. Stir the cornstarch mixture, then pour slowly into the pan and stir until the sauce thickens and is glossy, 1–2 minutes.

8 Transfer to a serving bowl or platter and serve right away with a side of rice.

This is Japan's national fried chicken dish, a standard appetizer or main course and great with beer. My husband is happy anytime I make it, and my youngest tries to beat everyone to the table so she will get a bigger share. I always make extra and hide it away to be eaten cold for lunch the next day. (For tips on deep-frying, see page 8.)

TORINIKU KARA-AGE

Fried Marinated Chicken

FOR THE MARINADE

1 cup soy sauce

1 small yellow onion, grated

2 teaspoons peeled and grated fresh ginger

2 teaspoons finely minced garlic

Canola or other neutral oil for deep-frying

1 pound boneless, skinless chicken thighs

1½ cups cornstarch

Lemon wedges

SERVES 4

1 To make the marinade, in a bowl, combine the soy sauce, onion, ginger, and garlic and stir well.

2 In a wok or deep, wide saucepan, pour 3 inches of oil and heat to 350°F on a deep-frying thermometer or until bubbles immediately form around a wooden chopstick held upright in the pan.

3 Trim any visible fat from the chicken thighs, then cut the meat diagonally about 1½ inches long and ¼-½ inch thick, using kitchen shears, if you like. Add the chicken to the marinade and let stand at room temperature for at least 10 minutes but no longer than 30 minutes or the chicken will toughen.

4 Spread the cornstarch in a large bowl. Working in batches to avoid crowding while deep-frying, remove several pieces of chicken from the marinade and drop into the cornstarch.

5 When the oil is ready, using tongs or wooden cooking chopsticks, lift the chicken out of the cornstarch, shaking off any excess, and carefully drop the chicken into the hot oil. If the oil bubbles excessively or foams, reduce the heat slightly. Cook, turning frequently with chopsticks or tongs to ensure even cooking, until the chicken is very brown and crisp, about 6 minutes. Transfer the chicken to a wire rack or paper towels to drain. Repeat until all the chicken is cooked. Discard the marinade.

6 Enjoy hot or at any temperature with lemon wedges.

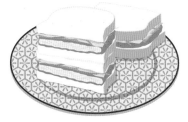

A juicy meat patty encased in a crispy *panko* coating and deep-fried is a guilty pleasure, but it is also one of Japan's most common lunch dishes, either slipped between bread slices spread with a little *tonkatsu* sauce for a sandwich or tucked into a *bento* (boxed lunch).

MENCHI KATSU

Crispy Panko-Fried Meat Patties

FOR THE MEAT MIXTURE

3 tablespoons *panko*
(page 161)

¼ cup whole or low-fat milk

1 tablespoon unsalted butter

1 yellow onion, minced

¾ pound ground beef

½ pound ground pork

1 large egg, lightly beaten

2 tablespoons mayonnaise

1½ teaspoons minced garlic

1 teaspoon brandy
(optional)

Pinch of salt

¼ teaspoon ground pepper

1 cup all-purpose flour

1 large egg

About 3 cups *panko*

Canola or other neutral oil
for deep-frying

Tonkatsu sauce (page 17)

SERVES 4

1 To make the meat mixture, in a bowl, mix together the *panko* and milk and set aside for 5 minutes. In a frying pan over medium heat, melt the butter. When the butter foams, add the onion and cook, stirring often, until translucent, 4–5 minutes. Remove from the heat and let cool. In a large bowl, combine the beef, pork, *panko* mixture, cooled onion, beaten egg, mayo, garlic, brandy (if using), salt, and pepper. Using your hands, mix well.

2 Spread the flour in a shallow bowl. Break the egg into a second shallow bowl and beat with chopsticks or a fork until well blended. Spread 2 cups of the *panko* in a third shallow bowl. Spread a little *panko* on a flat plate.

3 Dampen your hands and form the meat into patties about 3 inches wide and 1 inch thick. Gently dust each with the flour, shaking off any excess; coat with egg; then coat with the *panko*, adding more *panko* to the bowl as needed and lightly pressing the *panko* in place with your fingertips. Place each coated patty on the *panko*-lined plate.

4 In a wok or deep, wide saucepan, pour 3 inches of oil and heat to 350°F on a deep-frying thermometer or until a bit of *panko* dropped into the hot oil rises immediately to the surface. Working in batches to avoid crowding, drop the patties into the oil one at a time, and fry, turning 2 or 3 times, until the *panko* is golden brown and the meat is cooked through, about 6 minutes. Reduce the heat a bit if the patties brown too quickly. When cooked, using tongs, transfer the patties to a wire rack or paper towels to drain.

5 Serve the patties hot with a drizzle of *tonkatsu* sauce, or at room temperature as a sandwich with a little *tonkatsu* spread on untoasted white bread.

Another great recipe for the grill, this dish can be cooked as described here or *yakitori* style (see page 129) by cutting chicken into small pieces and threading them onto skewers. Serve as a main course with rice and green salad or with potato or macaroni salad.

TORINIKU NO MISOYAKI

Grilled Chicken with Miso Glaze

FOR THE MARINADE

1 tablespoon soy sauce

½ teaspoon sugar

1 tablespoon mirin

1 tablespoon sake

½ teaspoon peeled and grated fresh ginger

1 pound boneless, skinless chicken thighs, trimmed of visible fat and halved

FOR THE MISO GLAZE

1 tablespoon mirin

1 tablespoon sake

2 tablespoons sugar

¼ cup miso, preferably white

SERVES 2 OR 3

1   To make the marinade, in a shallow bowl large enough to accommodate the chicken in a single layer, stir together the soy sauce, sugar, mirin, sake, and ginger.

2   Add the chicken, turn to coat evenly, and let stand at room temperature for 15 minutes or up to 2 hours in the refrigerator. Prepare a medium fire in a charcoal or gas grill, or preheat the broiler.

3   To make the miso glaze, in a small bowl, stir together the mirin, sake, sugar, miso, and 3 tablespoons water and mix well. Set the glaze near the grill.

4   Transfer the chicken to the hottest part of the grill, discarding the marinade, and grill for 5 minutes. Turn the chicken, brush with some of the glaze, and grill for 5 minutes. Continue to grill, turning and brushing with the glaze every 5 minutes, until the chicken is cooked through, about 20 minutes total. Remove the chicken from the grill and serve hot, warm, or at room temperature.

This simple recipe is good with salt *(shio yakitori)* or with sauce *(tare yakitori)*. You can prepare half the recipe with the salt and half the recipe with the sauce to have the best of both worlds.

TORINIKU TO NEGI YAKITORI

Grilled Chicken & Onion Skewers

FOR THE BASTING SAUCE (OPTIONAL)

½ cup soy sauce

¼ cup mirin

2 tablespoons sugar

½ pound boneless, skinless chicken thighs, trimmed of visible fat and meat cut into bite-sized pieces

1 yellow onion, cut into 2-inch wedges

4–5 baby leeks, white part only, cut into 1-inch lengths (optional)

1 tablespoon canola or other neutral oil

Salt (optional)

MAKES 10 TO 12 SKEWERS

1 Submerge 10–12 bamboo skewers in water for at least 30 minutes before grilling. Prepare a medium-hot fire in a charcoal grill or a medium-high fire in a gas grill, or preheat the broiler.

2 To make the basting sauce (if using), in a small saucepan over medium-low heat, combine the soy sauce, mirin, and sugar and cook, stirring, until the sugar is dissolved and the liquid just begins to turn syrupy, 5–8 minutes. Remove from the heat and set aside in a small bowl.

3 Drain the skewers. Alternately thread pieces of chicken, onion, and leek (if using) onto the skewers. Brush the skewers lightly on all sides with the oil and place on a plate.

4 If using salt instead of the basting sauce, place the skewers over the hottest part of the grill and cook, turning 3 or 4 times, until the chicken is cooked through and the onions are scorched around the edges, about 5 minutes total. Sprinkle each skewer with salt and remove from the grill.

5 If using the basting sauce, dip each skewer in the sauce or brush the sauce onto the skewers. Place the skewers over the hottest part of the grill and cook, turning 3 or 4 times. Baste with additional sauce each time, until the chicken is cooked through and the onions are scorched around the edges, about 5 minutes total. Move the skewers to a cooler part of the grill if the sauce appears to burn.

6 Serve the skewers piping hot.

YAKITORI Walking down the alleys near the business districts in Tokyo, or beneath the noisy elevated train tracks, you will find whole villages of casual outdoor eating and drinking places, some of them no more than pushcarts or stalls with a couple of stools. These street stands, or *yatai*, each specialize in a different preparation, from *oden*, a stew-like dish made with fish cake, and *Yakisoba* (page 82), a delicious mix of noodles, vegetables, and meat fried on a griddle, to *yakitori*, grilled chicken skewers.

Stands offering *yakitori*, literally "burned chicken," give customers a wide array of choices, including thighs, wings, livers, hearts, and more. The skewers are basted with a sweet-and-savory soy-based glaze—the same sauce used for teriyaki—and are eaten simply, rarely with accompaniments other than a glass of beer and perhaps some *shichimi togarashi* (page 162) for sprinkling on the skewers. At home, you can serve the skewers as appetizers, or with a bowl of rice and a salad for a meal.

Found at *yatai* (see page 32) and on *izakaya* (see page 22) menus, this dish calls for only the simplest of ingredients and techniques. It is a terrific appetizer, and is perfect for casual parties. At my house, I use the largest, freshest chicken wings I can find, salt them liberally, and grill them until they are crispy and smoky but still juicy. I can't wait until they cool, and burn my tongue every time!

TEBASAKI

Grilled Chicken Wings

10–12 large chicken wings (see note)

Salt

Shichimi togarashi (page 162; optional)

SERVES 4

1 Pat the wings dry. Arrange on a tray or platter and refrigerate, uncovered, for 1 hour to dry further and produce a crispy skin.

2 Prepare a medium-hot fire in a charcoal grill or a medium-high fire in a gas grill, or preheat the broiler. Remove the wings from the refrigerator and salt them generously.

3 When the grill is ready, place the wings over the hottest part of the grill, cover, and cook, checking and turning every 5 minutes, until crispy and browned on both sides, about 15 minutes total.

4 Remove from the grill and serve piping hot. Sprinkle with the *shichimi togarashi*, if desired.

note: You can leave the wing tips intact, though some cooks cut them off because they find the tips burn easily.

This very homey recipe is a wonderful entry point to contemporary Japanese home cooking. *Amasu* literally means "sweet vinegar." These tasty little meatballs, made here with chicken, can also be made with ground pork or ground beef. Serve them as a main course, or make them for your next party and serve them, speared with toothpicks, at room temperature as appetizers.

TORINIKU DANGO NO AMASU AN

Chicken Meatballs with Sweet Vinegar Glaze

FOR THE SAUCE

¼ cup chicken broth

¼ cup soy sauce

¼ cup rice vinegar

1 tablespoon ketchup

1 tablespoon Worcestershire sauce

3 tablespoons sugar

1 tablespoon cornstarch

2 tablespoons canola or other neutral oil

Ground chicken mixture (see *Tsukune*, page 134), shaped into 1-inch balls

SERVES 4

1 To make the sauce, in a small bowl, stir together the broth, soy sauce, vinegar, ketchup, Worcestershire sauce, and sugar until the sugar is dissolved. Place near the stove. In another small bowl, stir together the cornstarch and 2 tablespoons water, mix well, and place near the stove.

2 In a frying pan large enough to hold the meatballs in a single layer, warm the oil over medium-high heat. When the oil is hot, add the meatballs and cook, gently shaking the pan to turn them so they cook evenly, until cooked through, about 5 minutes. Reduce the heat to medium and pour in the sauce. Continue to cook, shaking the pan to distribute the sauce, until the meatballs are evenly coated and the sauce bubbles, watching that the sauce does not burn, about 3 minutes. Stir the cornstarch-water mixture, then pour it into the pan, shaking the pan to distribute it evenly, and cook until the sauce thickens slightly, 30–60 seconds.

3 Transfer the meatballs and the sauce to a platter or individual plates and serve hot or at room temperature.

One of my favorite *yakitori* (see page 129), this same ground chicken mixture is used in *Chankonabe* (page 138) and *Toriniku Dango no Amasu An* (page 132). Plus, I've shaped this mixture into patties for teriyaki chicken "hamburgers." This dish can be served cold with cooked rice and potato croquettes (page 57), potato salad (page 66), or macaroni salad (see note page 67).

TSUKUNE

Grilled Ground Chicken Meatballs

FOR THE BASTING SAUCE

½ cup soy sauce

¼ cup mirin

2 tablespoons sugar

FOR THE GROUND CHICKEN MIXTURE

½ pound ground chicken

1 large egg, beaten and then halved

2 teaspoons ginger juice (see page 157)

2 teaspoons soy sauce

1 tablespoon cornstarch

About 6 tablespoons *panko* (page 161)

3 tablespoons finely chopped green onion, including tender green tops

Canola or other neutral oil

MAKES 10 SKEWERS

1 Submerge 10-12 bamboo skewers in water about 30 minutes before grilling.

2 To make the sauce, in a small saucepan over medium-low heat, combine the soy sauce, mirin, and sugar and cook, stirring, until the sugar is dissolved and the liquid just begins to turn syrupy, 5-8 minutes. Set aside in a small bowl.

3 To make the ground chicken mixture, in a large bowl, combine the chicken, ½ beaten egg (reserve the remaining egg for another use), the ginger juice, soy sauce, cornstarch, *panko*, and green onion. Using your hands, mix until well combined. Sprinkle with *panko* as needed to shape the mixture into a ball.

4 Prepare a medium-hot fire in a charcoal grill or a medium-high fire in a gas grill, or preheat the broiler. Drain the skewers. Moisten your hands. Holding a skewer, take a clump of chicken mixture and form a cylinder on the skewer by packing it in place. Carefully lay the completed skewers on a large plate.

5 Brush the grill grate lightly with oil. Place the skewers over the hottest part of the grill. Grill until the first side changes color, about 1 minute. Carefully grab the meat to turn the skewers, so the meat stays in place, and cook the second side. Generously baste the top of each skewer with sauce. When the second side has changed color and the meat has set, about 1 minute, turn the skewers and baste the second side with sauce. Continue turning the skewers and basting with sauce until the chicken is cooked through, 5-7 minutes, moving the skewers to a cooler part of the grill if the sauce appears to burn.

6 Serve hot, at room temperature, or cold with side dishes.

This dish was inspired by a *bento* I ate on a train ride in southern Honshu, Japan's main island. At one station, we found a terrific array of *bento* boxes, and nearly missed the train as I agonized over which one to try. I picked the *iridori* and spent the next few hours trying to decipher the ingredients so I could re-create it at home.

IRIDORI

Simmered Chicken & Vegetables

½ cup trimmed and halved green beans or snow peas

5 tablespoons mirin

5 tablespoons sake

3 tablespoons soy sauce

2 tablespoons sugar

1 carrot

1 parsnip

1 tablespoon canola or other neutral oil

1 tablespoon sesame oil

½ pound ground chicken

4 fresh shiitake mushrooms, stem removed and caps quartered

½ cup sliced bamboo shoots

Salt

SERVES 2

1 Fill a small saucepan with water and bring to a boil. Add the green beans and blanch for 1 minute. Drain and immediately rinse under running cold water to halt the cooking. Place near the stove. In a small bowl, stir together the mirin, sake, soy sauce, and sugar until the sugar is dissolved. Place near the stove. Peel the carrot and parsnip, halve lengthwise, and cut crosswise into ¼-inch-thick half-moons.

2 In a large frying pan over medium-high heat, warm the canola and sesame oils. When they are hot, swirl to coat the bottom and sides of the pan. Add the chicken, breaking it up well with a spatula. Cook, stirring, until half cooked, about 3 minutes. Add the mushrooms, bamboo shoots, carrot, and parsnip and cook, stirring, until the chicken is cooked through and the vegetables have started to soften, 5–7 minutes. Add the mirin mixture, mix well, and reduce the heat to medium. Continue to cook, stirring occasionally, until the vegetables are tender, about 5 minutes longer.

3 Season to taste with salt, add the green beans, stir to mix, and heat through. Transfer to a serving bowl or platter and serve.

Chankonabe is just one of many variations on *nabemono* (one-pot dishes). It is traditionally eaten by sumo wrestlers as a way to put on the amount of weight they need for their sport. Don't be afraid that you will turn into a sumo wrestler if you eat this stew, however.

CHANKONABE

Sumo Wrestler's Stew

FOR THE STEW

Ground chicken mixture
(see *Tsukune*, page 134),
shaped into 1-inch balls

1½ pounds cod fillet, cut
into 2-inch chunks; shrimp,
peeled and deveined;
and/or shucked oysters

6 ounces thick-cut sliced
bacon, cut into 2-inch pieces

4 boneless, skinless chicken
thighs, trimmed of visible
fat and meat and cut into
bite-sized pieces

1 package (14 ounces) medium
tofu, cut into 1-inch cubes

½ head Napa cabbage,
leaves separated and large
leaves halved

2 leeks, white part only,
halved lengthwise and
cut diagonally into 1-inch-
thick pieces

6 green onions, including
tender green tops, cut into
2-inch lengths

1 To ready the stew ingredients, place the meatballs, seafood, bacon, chicken, tofu, cabbage, leeks, green onions, and mushrooms on platters near the stove if you are cooking the stew ingredients there or on the table if you are using a portable gas burner.

2 Pour the *ponzu* sauce and *goma dare* into individual dipping bowls at each place setting along with chopsticks, a soup spoon (optional), and a soup bowl.

3 To make the broth, in a Dutch oven or other large pot over medium heat, combine the broth, sake, mirin, ginger juice, and garlic and bring to a simmer. Spoon several spoonfuls of broth into a small bowl, add the miso, and stir until smooth. Gradually add the miso mixture to the broth in the pot, stirring to avoid lumps. Once the miso has been incorporated, do not let the broth boil.

4 If cooking the stew ingredients on the stove top, cook in batches. Add some of each of the ingredients to the broth, simmer (do not boil) until cooked, and serve them, returning to the stove to start a new batch as each previous batch is eaten.

The wrestlers eat much bigger portions—so big that they typically take a nap immediately after they leave the table, which helps them pack on the pounds. Dipping sauces are often provided, with *ponzu* (a citrus sauce) and *goma dare* (a sesame sauce) popular choices.

4-6 fresh shiitake mushrooms, stems removed and caps quartered or white mushrooms, stems trimmed and caps quartered

Ponzu sauce (page 16)

Goma dare (page 16)

FOR THE BROTH

6 cups chicken broth

¼ cup sake

⅓ cup plus 1 tablespoon mirin

2 tablespoons ginger juice (page 157)

1½ teaspoons crushed garlic

½ cup miso, preferably white

4-6 cups cooked udon noodles (1 cup per person), or 2-3 cups cooked rice (see *Gohan*, page 73; ½ cup per person)

SERVES 4-6

5 If cooking the stew ingredients at the table, make the broth on the stove top and pour it into the *nabe*. Add all of the ingredients at the same time, with diners selecting them as they are cooked (the vegetables and tofu cook more quickly than the meatballs, seafood, and chicken).

6 Keep the broth at a simmer the entire time. If the liquid gets low, add a little water or chicken broth to have enough liquid to heat the noodles or rice at the end (even though you are thinning the broth, the flavorful ingredients you are cooking in it continue to enrich it).

7 When diners are ready, remove any solids in the broth and add the noodles or rice. Simmer until heated through, then ladle into the soup bowls and serve.

note: If you want to try this dish, but you don't have a gas burner, you can cook the stew on the stove top, transfer it to a large bowl, and serve it family style.

In the town near Tokyo where I lived, there was a small restaurant across the street from the train station. Its sign read "24 Hours Open" and had a picture of one dish only: the beef bowl. I had no idea what "beef bowl" was, but I could read the price—cheap. I had my first one and like millions of other office workers, I was hooked.

GYUDON

Sweet Simmered Beef & Onions over Rice

½ pound beef rib eye

2 tablespoons unsalted butter

½ large yellow onion, thinly sliced

1 tablespoon sake

⅓ cup plus 2 tablespoons white wine

1¼ cups water

3 tablespoons soy sauce

½ teaspoon ginger juice (see page 157)

2 tablespoons sugar

¼ teaspoon very finely minced garlic

½ teaspoon salt

2 cups hot cooked rice (see *Gohan*, page 73)

2 large eggs for serving (see note; optional)

2 tablespoons *beni shoga* for serving (optional)

SERVES 2

1 Freeze the beef for 1 hour before very thinly slicing it (almost shaving it).

2 In a saucepan over medium heat, melt the butter. When the butter foams, add the onion and cook, stirring often, until translucent, 4-5 minutes. Add the sake and wine and cook for about 2 minutes. Add the water, soy sauce, ginger juice, sugar, garlic, and salt and mix well. Add the beef and cook, stirring constantly to prevent the pieces from sticking together, until just cooked through, 2-3 minutes.

3 Divide the rice between 2 bowls and spoon the beef mixture on top. If you like, provide an egg per person to be cracked and mixed into the hot beef and rice with a tablespoon of the *beni shoga* on the side, if using.

note: There is a low risk for exposure to salmonella bacteria in raw eggs, but the elderly, the very young, pregnant women, and anyone who is ill or has a compromised immune system should not consume raw eggs.

Hamburg epitomizes the *yoshoku* concept—the perfect example of a Western dish adapted to Japanese taste. It is a bit like meat loaf, but it is transformed by the rich sauce. I use a combination of beef and pork for texture and richness. A Japanese coffeehouse touch is to serve it with a fried egg atop.

HAMBURG

Japanese-Style Hamburger Steak

FOR THE HAMBURGER STEAKS

⅓ cup *panko* (page 161)

¼ cup whole or low-fat milk

3 tablespoons canola or other neutral oil

1 small yellow onion, minced

¾ pound ground beef

¼ pound ground pork

1 medium egg, lightly beaten

Salt and freshly ground pepper

2 tablespoons sake

1 cup *Hamburg So-su* (page 17)

SERVES 4

1 To make the hamburger steaks, in a small bowl, mix together the *panko* and milk and set aside for 5 minutes. In a small frying pan over medium heat, warm 1 tablespoon of the oil. When the oil is hot, add the onion and cook, stirring often, until lightly browned, 5–7 minutes. Remove from the heat and let cool completely. In a large bowl, combine the beef, pork, *panko* mixture, cooled onion, egg, ½ teaspoon salt, and ¼ teaspoon pepper. Using your hands, combine well, then gather the mixture into a large mass and slap it back into the bowl a few times to help create dense patties without interior air bubbles that might cause them to break apart during cooking. Divide the meat into 4 equal portions and form each into a patty about 1½ inches thick.

2 In a frying pan large enough to accommodate the patties without crowding or working in 2 batches, heat the remaining 2 tablespoons oil or half of the oil per batch over medium-high heat. When the oil is hot, carefully add the patties and cook until a browned crust starts to form on the bottoms, 4–5 minutes. Carefully turn the patties and cook until a browned crust starts to form on the second sides, 4–5 minutes longer.

3 Add 1 tablespoon of the sake per side (or ½ tablespoon per side per batch) to the pan, cover, and cook for 2 minutes. Uncover, carefully turn the patties, add the remaining sake, cover, and cook until the patties are very brown on the outside and cooked through, about 2 minutes longer. As soon as the patties are done, uncover the pan, pour in the *Hamburg So-su*, and turn the patties once to coat both sides with the sauce. Cook until the patties are well coated and the sauce is hot, 1–2 minutes longer.

4 Transfer to individual plates and serve right away.

This hearty, savory, beefy, tomatoey recipe is a *yoshoku* dish—dishes that are commonly adopted from French, Italian, and even American cuisine. They are Western in both presentation and many ingredients, which makes *yoshoku* dishes great to re-create at home.

HAYASHI RAISU

Beef & Onions in Tomato Gravy over Rice

¾ pound beef rib eye

Salt and freshly ground pepper

1 teaspoon plus
1 tablespoon sugar

3 tablespoons unsalted butter

1½ yellow onions, cut into ¼-inch-thick slices

½ cup sliced white mushrooms

2½ tablespoons all-purpose flour

1 cup dry red wine

¾ cup tomato purée

3 tablespoons Worcestershire sauce

1 chicken or beef bouillon cube, or ½ teaspoon granulated chicken stock base

3-4 cups hot cooked rice (see *Gohan*, page 73)

SERVES 4

1 Freeze the beef for 1 hour before very thinly slicing it (almost shaving it). Place the beef in a large bowl and sprinkle with ½ teaspoon salt, ½ teaspoon pepper, and the 1 teaspoon sugar. Using your hands, massage the seasonings evenly into the beef. Set aside.

2 In a large frying pan or a wok over medium-high heat, melt 2 tablespoons of the butter. When the butter foams, add the onions and cook, stirring often, until translucent and soft but not browned, 4-6 minutes. Transfer the onions to a Dutch oven or other heavy pot.

3 Add the remaining 1 tablespoon butter to the frying pan over medium-high heat. When the butter foams, add the meat and cook briefly, stirring constantly to prevent the pieces from sticking together. Add the mushrooms. When the beef is almost cooked, about 3 minutes, sprinkle in the flour and mix well. Add the wine, stir well, and transfer to the pot with the onions.

4 Place the pot over medium-high heat and heat until the mixture bubbles. Reduce the heat to medium-low, add the tomato purée, the remaining 1 tablespoon sugar, the Worcestershire sauce, and the bouillon cube and mix well. Cook, uncovered, until the flavors are blended, about 15 minutes.

5 Season to taste with salt and pepper. Serve hot on one side of each plate with a serving of rice on the other.

Although I have no sisters of my own, I gained one through marriage, Mayumi. This is one of her standards because it comes together quickly from what is on hand. You can substitute ground pork or chicken for the beef, along with any number of vegetables. Top it with a fried sunny-side-up egg for an authentic Japanese presentation.

ONEESAN NO DURAI KARE

My Sister-in-Law's Spicy Ground Beef & Vegetable "Dry" Curry

3 tablespoons mirin

2 tablespoons sake

¼ cup soy sauce

1 teaspoon salt

5 teaspoons curry powder

2 fresh shiitake mushrooms

1 small carrot

1 yellow onion

½ green bell pepper

2 tablespoons unsalted butter

¾ pound ground beef

½ cup fresh or frozen corn kernels

1 teaspoon red pepper flakes

¼ teaspoon paprika

¼ apple, cored, peeled, and grated (optional)

3-4 cups hot cooked rice (see *Gohan*, page 73)

SERVES 4

1 In a small bowl, combine the mirin, sake, ¼ cup water, soy sauce, salt, and curry powder and mix well. Set aside.

2 Remove and discard the stems from the mushrooms and mince the caps. Peel and finely chop the carrot, mince the onion, and seed and mince the bell pepper.

3 In a large frying pan or wok over medium-high heat, melt the butter. When it foams, add the beef and cook, breaking it up with a spatula or spoon, until it has lost most of its redness, 3-4 minutes. Add the mushrooms, carrot, onion, bell pepper, corn, red pepper flakes, and paprika and cook, stirring constantly, until the onion, carrot, and bell pepper have softened, about 5 minutes. Add the mirin mixture and the apple (if using) and cook, stirring constantly, until the liquid is absorbed, 3-4 minutes longer.

4 Serve the curry piping hot on individual plates with a mound of rice alongside.

A thick, mild-or-spicy classic based on English-style curry, *kare raisu* is arguably the best-known dish in Japan's large repertoire of "borrowed" cuisine. After its introduction in the late 1870s, curry rice became a hugely popular dish in universities and other schools, at lunch counters, and in homes.

KARE RAISU

Curry Rice

3 tablespoons unsalted butter

5 tablespoons curry powder

2 large yellow onions, thinly sliced

1½ teaspoons minced garlic

1½ teaspoons peeled and minced fresh ginger

1 teaspoon red pepper flakes

1 bay leaf

2 tablespoons all-purpose flour

1 pound boneless stewing beef, cut into 1-inch cubes

1 tablespoon canola or other neutral oil

1 tomato, halved, seeded, and chopped

2 cups chicken broth

2 small russet potatoes, peeled and cut into 1½-inch chunks

1 large carrot, peeled and cut into 1-inch chunks

1 teaspoon salt

1 In a Dutch oven or other heavy pot over medium-high heat, melt 2 tablespoons of the butter. Add 2½ tablespoons of the curry powder and half of the onion slices, stir well, cover, and cook, stirring every 2 minutes or so to prevent scorching, until the onions are medium brown, about 10 minutes. Stir in the garlic, ginger, red pepper flakes, and bay leaf and stir to combine.

2 Meanwhile, spread the flour in a shallow bowl and lightly dust the beef cubes, shaking off any excess. In a large frying pan over medium-high heat, warm the oil. When the oil is hot, working in batches to avoid crowding, add the beef cubes and brown on all sides, 3–4 minutes. Add the browned beef and the tomato to the curry mixture and mix well. Pour in the broth. Bring to a simmer over medium heat and cook the curry, uncovered, for 15 minutes.

3 Meanwhile, rinse the frying pan, return to medium heat, and add the remaining 1 tablespoon butter. When the butter foams, add the potato and carrot and cook, stirring, for about 2 minutes. After the curry has cooked for

Continued on page 148

Continued from page 147

The thick, rich sauce is often served over *Tonkatsu* (page 110) or *Ebi Furai* (page 102) with rice on the side. Eaten with a spoonful of rice to soak up every last bit of flavor, it is real Japanese comfort food. Yogurt and grated apple are my secret flavorings.

2 tablespoons Worcestershire sauce

½ small apple, peeled, cored, and grated (optional)

Yogurt (optional)

4-5 cups hot cooked rice (see *Gohan*, page 73)

***Fukujinzuke* red pickle, specifically for curry (optional)**

SERVES 6

15 minutes, add the potato and carrot chunks, the remaining 2½ tablespoons curry powder, the remaining onion slices, and the salt and stir well. Reduce the heat to medium-low, cover, and cook until the potatoes are soft but have not disintegrated and the carrot and beef are tender, about 20 minutes longer.

4   Remove from the heat and stir in the Worcestershire sauce. Add the apple and yogurt, if using, and stir well. Divide the rice among 6 bowls, arranging the rice in a half-moon on one side of each bowl and the curry in the other half, overlapping the rice so that every bite (with a spoon!) contains both rice and curry. Serve with a teaspoonful of *fukujinzuke*, if using.

DEPARCHIKA

The *deparchika* (department-store basement floor) is a central element in the complex world of Japanese food. It is traditionally filled with individual "shops"—glass counters or mini food stalls—offering a different specialty, from tempura, sushi, and potato croquettes to German sausages, Korean kimchee, and Chinese noodles. Plus, there is always a big supermarket packed with fresh fish, meat, and vegetables. Famous restaurants often have small take-out operations featuring a signature dish, and bakery stands rival their street-address competition with a wide array of sweets, both Japanese and Western (particularly French).

The quality of the prepared foods is universally exceptional, with prices to match. Tastings of some of the items (usually seaweed, dried fish, pickled plums, and other bite-sized delicacies, but not those behind the counters) are offered freely, particularly to curious and adventurous (and polite) foreigners. Housewives rushed for time regularly purchase an entire meal—appetizer, main dish, side dishes, dessert, even a bottle of wine—for a quick but pricey dinner solution.

The recipes for this favorite home-style meat-and-potato stew vary widely. Everyone's mother has a "secret" recipe, and the taste can be quite different from region to region and even house to house. This recipe combines my mother-in-law's version with a few embellishments to satisfy my family's tastes.

NIKU JAGA

Sweet Simmered Beef & Potatoes

½ pound beef sirloin

1 tablespoon rice vinegar or white vinegar

3 large russet potatoes

1 tablespoon canola or other neutral oil

1 large yellow onion, thinly sliced

3 tablespoons mirin

2 tablespoons sake

1½ tablespoons sugar

5 tablespoons soy sauce

10-20 snow peas, slivered, for garnish

SERVES 4

1 Freeze the beef for 1 hour before very thinly slicing it (almost shaving it).

2 Add the vinegar to a large bowl of water. Peel the potatoes and cut each into 8 equal chunks. Immediately immerse the potatoes in the vinegar water to prevent darkening. Rinse and drain the potatoes just before using.

3 In a Dutch oven or other heavy pot over medium heat, warm the oil. When the oil is hot, add the beef and cook, stirring constantly to prevent the pieces from sticking, just until it turns color, about 2 minutes. Add the potatoes to the pan with half of the onion slices, then pour in enough water just to cover. Bring to a simmer, cover, reduce the heat to medium-low, and cook until a skewer or chopstick inserted into a potato easily pierces about ¼ inch, about 15 minutes.

4 Add the mirin, sake, sugar, soy sauce, and the remaining onion slices, stir briefly to mix, cover with a drop-lid (page 11), and cook over medium heat until the potatoes are cooked through, about 10 minutes longer.

5 Meanwhile, trim the snow peas. Have ready a bowl of ice water. Blanch the peas in boiling water for 1 minute, drain, and immerse in the ice water until chilled through. Drain again.

6 Serve the stew hot on a platter or in individual bowls and garnish with the snow peas.

One of the best-known Japanese dishes in the West, *sukiyaki* gained popularity in Japan in the late 1800s, when the government started to promote beef after a centuries-long ban on eating it. This dish is a favorite of men (meat) and kids (sweet).

SUKIYAKI

Paper-Thin Beef, Green Onions & Vegetables in Sweet Soy Sauce

1 pound beef sirloin
or other well-marbled beef

1 package (14 ounces)
firm tofu

4½ tablespoons canola
or other neutral oil

FOR THE SAUCE

1 cup soy sauce

1 cup mirin

2 cups sake

About 3 tablespoons sugar

3 leeks, white parts
only, cut diagonally into
½-inch-thick pieces

1 small yellow onion, halved
through the stem end and
cut into ¼-inch-thick slices

6 fresh shiitake mushrooms,
stems removed and caps
halved

1 Freeze the beef for 1 hour before very thinly slicing it (almost shaving it).

2 Place several layers of paper towels on a cutting board and place the tofu on it. Top with several paper towels, then top with a plate and a weight, such as a can of tomatoes. Let drain for 15 minutes, then very carefully replace all of the paper towels and let drain for another 15 minutes. Remove the weight and the paper towels and pat the tofu dry.

3 Heat a ridged stove-top grill pan over high heat. When the pan is hot, add ½ tablespoon of the oil. When the oil is hot, add the tofu and cook, turning only once, until both sides have dark brown grill marks, 4-5 minutes per side. Remove from the heat, let cool, and cut into 1½-inch cubes.

4 To make the sauce, in a bowl, stir together the soy sauce, mirin, sake, and sugar, starting with 3 tablespoons and adding more to taste, until the sugar is dissolved. Set aside.

5 Heat a large nonstick frying pan over medium-high heat. When the pan is hot, add 1 tablespoon of the oil. When the oil is hot, working in 4 batches, add one-fourth of the meat, then one-fourth each of the tofu, leeks, yellow onion,

Continued on page 152

Continued from page 151

Japanese accompany *sukiyaki* with a small dish of beaten raw egg for dipping the sweet beef. In the US, many people have an aversion to eating raw egg, either fearing it might carry harmful bacteria or because they don't like the consistency. If you have a source for good, fresh eggs, you should give the egg a try, making sure you beat it well. The hot beef will cook the egg a little, the egg will cool down the meat a little, and the richness of the combined taste will be a pleasant surprise.

6 green onions, including tender green tops, cut diagonally into 2-inch pieces

½ head Napa cabbage, cut into 1-inch squares

4 medium or large eggs (see note, page 141) or *ponzu* sauce (page 16) for serving

SERVES 4

mushrooms, green onions, and cabbage. Using a ladle, stir the sauce, then ladle a generous amount of sauce into the pan so it bubbles a bit. Cook the ingredients in the sauce, browning the tofu and wilting the cabbage, onion, and leeks, 5–6 minutes. Transfer the contents to an individual bowl, serving each batch hot as it is cooked, and repeat with the remaining ingredients and oil to make 3 more servings. (If you have an extra-large *sukiyaki* pan, cook in 1 batch and reduce the oil to 2½ tablespoons.)

6 Provide each diner with a well-beaten raw egg in a small bowl, if using, or with a little *ponzu* sauce for dipping.

note: *Sukiyaki* calls for *yakidofu*, "grilled tofu," which is available in packages at Japanese and Asian markets. However, it is easy to make yourself.

Shabu Shabu, named for the "swish swish" sound of dragging the meat in the water to cook it, is a really fun group meal. Many restaurants have built-in table burners, but making it at home is just as easy, especially if you have a tabletop burner. There's little prep, and cooking in the broth makes it an easy and healthy meal.

SHABU SHABU

"Swish Swish" Beef Hotpot

About 6 cups kombu dashi, dashi (page 156), or water

2 packages (14 ounces each) soft, medium, or firm tofu

10 green onions

1 package (8 ounces) *shimeji* mushrooms

½ head Napa cabbage, leaves separated and quartered

4 cups spinach or arugula leaves, rinsed and patted dry

8-10 shiitake mushrooms, stems removed and each cap lightly scored with a cross

1 carrot, peeled and cut into thin rounds

2 pounds sirloin, rib eye, or other well-marbled beef, sliced paper thin

Ponzu sauce (page 16), *goma dare* sauce (page 16), and *shichimi togarashi* (page 162) for serving

1 package (8-10 ounces) frozen or dried udon noodles

SERVES 2

1 In a large cooking pot over medium heat, bring the broth to a simmer on the stove top. Place a large *nabe*, earthenware pot, or enameled cast-iron pot on a portable gas burner in the center of the dining table and pour the simmering broth into it, filling it three-fourths full.

2 Cut the tofu into 2-inch cubes, and slice the green onions diagonally into 1½-inch lengths. Remove the large part of the stem from the *shimeji* mushrooms and pull them apart. Place the vegetables, tofu, and raw meat on large platters and set around the burner along with the sauces and *shichimi togarashi*. Set each place setting with individual dipping bowls, chopsticks, a soup spoon (optional), and a soup bowl.

3 Add some of each vegetable and some tofu to the simmering broth, letting them cook for a few minutes before diners select, dip, and eat them. Using chopsticks, ask diners to select a piece of meat and swirl it in the broth (swish swish, don't let go!) just until it turns color, about 1 minute, then dip it into the sauce of their choice and eat it. If the liquid gets low, add a little water to have enough liquid to heat the udon.

4 When diners are ready, skim off any scum from the soup, add the udon and cook until soft, serving it as noodle soup, seasoned to taste with salt and pepper, to end the meal.

Ingredients

I have written these recipes so you can create the authentic flavor of home-style Japanese dishes using ingredients available, for the most part, in supermarkets. Since this book is focused on popular, everyday Japanese cooking, exotic ingredients are not essential. You will discover that many of these contemporary, family-friendly dishes are simply interesting uses of familiar foods, rather than combinations of exotic ingredients. And since many are based on Japanese adaptations from other cuisines, I think they are particularly accessible. If you have trouble finding any of the ingredients, check the Sources section (page 163) for online possibilities.

BAMBOO SHOOTS Crunchy and mild in flavor, boiled bamboo shoots appear in soups, stir-fries, and more and are sold canned or in plastic packs, whole and sliced. If whole, cone-shaped shoots, they can easily be sliced for most recipes. Rinse under running cold water before using.

BENI SHOGA See Ginger.

CABBAGE Regular green cabbage *(cabegi)* is used in many modern Japanese dishes. To use, remove and discard the outer layer of leaves and cut as directed in individual recipes. When a recipe calls for shredded cabbage, if you can find it, the angel hair cabbage sold in bags in the supermarket is an excellent timesaver. See also Napa Cabbage.

CHILI BEAN PASTE See Sauces.

CORNSTARCH *Katakuriko,* originally made from the root of the dogtooth violet and now made from the considerably less exotic Irish potato, is a thickener for cooked sauces. Cornstarch is a good substitute. It is mixed with water in varying ratios, depending on the dish, and then added near the end of cooking. Always stir the mixture again briefly just before using and add it slowly, stirring it into the dish until the desired consistency is achieved. Cornstarch is also a good

coating for meat or chicken for deep-frying (see *Toriniku Kara-age,* page 123), yielding crispy results.

CUCUMBER The cucumber *(kyuri)* grown in Japan has dense flesh, thin skin, and few seeds. You can use English or hothouse cucumbers in its place and leave the skin on.

DAIKON This long (10 to 20 inches), creamy white, fat, mild and crisp radish is a common ingredient in all types of Japanese dishes. It is eaten raw, pickled, and simmered in soups and braises.

Choose firm daikon with smooth, unwrinkled skin. Peel before using. Grated daikon is used in dipping sauces for noodles and tempura and other fried foods (it is believed to aid in digestion) and is served with certain types of grilled fish. To grate, use any fine-rasp grater or an *oroshi* (page 11). Grated daikon releases a lot of water, which you must squeeze out by hand before serving. Red radishes have a sharper flavor than daikon, but they can be peeled and used if daikon is unavailable.

DASHI At the heart of many Japanese recipes, dashi is stock made from dried bonito flakes or dried anchovies or sardines. Many types of dashi exist, but for the most part, the modern Japanese home cook uses d*ashi-no-*

moto, instant dashi in powder, granule, or tea-bag form. *Dashi-no-moto* is available in Asian markets and by mail order, but you can also buy it at many Western markets. There are also instant granules marketed under the name *hondashi*, which is usually a soup base made from bonito flakes and kombu, a type of kelp.

I recommend that you use any basic *katsuo* (bonito) dashi. All types of instant dashi keep well—like chicken bouillon—and only a small amount is used for each recipe, so if you cannot pick it up easily at a local store, mail order a supply to have on hand. It is essential for making authentic-tasting miso soup and many other recipes and is the one Japanese ingredient that I encourage you to seek out. I have tried to substitute chicken broth for dashi where possible, but in the recipes where dashi still appears, you can use canned chicken or vegetable broth in its place, but the results will not be as authentic.

EDAMAME These fresh soybeans in fuzzy green pods are a popular snack food, especially as an accompaniment to beer or sake. Eat the beans only, of course, by forcing them from the pod with your lips directly into your mouth. Although I don't call for them in any recipe, edamame are easy to prepare (cook the frozen ones according to the package directions and boil the fresh ones in generously salted water for about 10 minutes).

EGGPLANT The best type to use is the long, slender, deep purple Japanese eggplant, although long, lavender Chinese eggplants are fine, too. Both have denser flesh and far fewer seeds than larger varieties.

Choose firm, unblemished eggplants with no discoloration or soft spots. If you must use a large globe eggplant, slice it into rounds or sticks, and discard the section with the most seeds, which could make dishes look dark and unappealing.

My recipes often call for frying the eggplant in oil first by itself and then cooking it in a sauce, which creates a soft texture and a rich taste. It is best not to fry eggplants straight from the refrigerator because cold eggplants soak up more oil than room-temperature eggplants.

GINGER Fresh ginger *(shoga)* is easily found in most supermarkets. Look for creamy, smooth yellow or tan skin.

Most of my recipes call for grated ginger or ginger juice. Grated or minced ginger is sometimes available in convenient jars, which must be stored in the refrigerator after opening. To grate your own ginger, peel away the thin skin with a paring knife or vegetable peeler and then run the flesh across a fine-rasp grater, either a Japanese *oroshi* (page 11) or a handheld Western grater. Always cut a piece about an inch longer than you need to avoid nicking your fingers on the sharp rasps. Grating ginger can be a chore, but you usually need only a small amount, so it is done fairly quickly. To extract ginger juice, you don't need to peel the ginger. Simply grate it and then squeeze the pulp in your hand to release the juice. A three-inch piece of fresh ginger yields about 2 teaspoons juice.

When making soups with meat, a Japanese cook often slips a large slice of unpeeled ginger into the broth to reduce the "meaty" smell that would otherwise fill the typically small Japanese kitchen.

Beni shoga (pickled ginger): Bright pink, sharp-flavored, vinegary matchsticks of marinated ginger, it is sometimes stocked in the refrigerated Asian section of Western markets (with the dumpling wrappers and tofu). Do not mistake *beni shoga* for *gari*, the pale marinated ginger served with sushi.

Beni shoga is used in small amounts—no more than a teaspoon or two—to garnish *Hiyashi Chuka* (page 85), *Yakisoba* (page 82), and in some types of ramen. The vinegary ginger provides a nice contrast to the richness. It is also sometimes mixed into the batter for *Okonomiyaki* (page 30) and *Takoyaki* (page 32).

GOMA DARE See Sauces.

GREEN ONION Green onions *(negi)* are used extensively in Japanese cooking. Though similar in flavor to the green onions found in Western markets, the Japanese *negi* is closer in size to a thin leek. Western green onions are a perfect substitute—I have used them for the recipes in this book. In most cases, you will use the white part and all but the very top of the green parts. Usually I wash the onion, peel off and discard the outer layer, slice the onion in half lengthwise, and then mince or thinly slice it crosswise.

HOT CHILI OIL See Oils.

ICHIMI TOGARASHI See *Shichimi togarashi and Ichimi togarashi.*

KABOCHA PUMPKIN This round, heavy gourd, known as both a pumpkin and a squash, has green-and-white mottled skin, dense orange flesh, and a sweet full flavor. Because the skin is very hard, you will need to use a large, heavy knife to cut the squash into chunks. When cooked, the skin is completely edible, so my recipes call for removing the stem and seeds, but not peeling the pumpkin.

KARASHI This Chinese-style hot yellow mustard powder *(karashi)* is easy to find. Most powdered mustards are mixed in a ratio of 2 teaspoons mustard powder to 1 tablespoon water, but check the package for directions. This condiment is served in a little dab to accompany *tonkatsu* or other fried dishes or for mixing with *Hiyashi Chuka* (page 85). It's pretty hot, so taste it before you start mixing it in.

MAYONNAISE Mayonnaise is mixed with other ingredients in some recipes in this book, including the pumpkin *korokke* (croquettes; page 54) and the crispy meat patties (page 124). When used in this way, the mayonnaise helps maintain juiciness and adds richness without the actual taste of mayonnaise. However, Japanese do love to use mayonnaise in salads and as a condiment. Japanese mayonnaise has a particular flavor, more acidic than the eggy richness of its European or Western counterparts. You can either buy

Japanese mayonnaise online (I like Kewpie brand; my husband always brings home several squeeze bottles from his trips to Japan) or use regular mayonnaise.

MEATS I have included many modern, Western-inspired recipes in this book that use a good deal more meat than you might expect for Japanese food. Meat is, of course, widely available and regularly used in Japanese cooking today, but because it typically is only one element of the dish, rather than the focus, it is often ground or very thinly sliced.

Some of my chicken recipes call for ground chicken. I use dark meat only, as it contributes good flavor and succulence. Sometimes it is difficult to find ground chicken, but Asian markets almost always have it. You can grind your own in a food processor, using boneless, skinless thighs (or ask your butcher to do it). For other recipes, I have specified boneless, skinless chicken thigh meat.

I also use a lot of ground pork in my recipes. It is rich tasting and juicy, lends itself well to some of the spicier dishes, and provides an extra flavor element when mixed with ground beef. If you can't find ground pork, ask your butcher to grind pork tenderloin or pork loin for you or grind your own in a food processor.

In addition, many of the soups and stir-fries call for a tender, fatty pork cut known as *baraniku*, literally "belly meat." This is not easy to find outside of Japan except in Japanese, Korean, or Chinese markets. As an alternative, I have used thick-cut bacon in many recipes. You can also use boneless pork shoulder: freeze it partially for an hour or so, and use a sharp knife and some muscle power to almost shave it.

Japanese cattle, grain-fed, massaged beer drinkers that they are, produce some of the most delectable, delicately rich, beefy-tasting meat in the world. I do not cook with that and neither will you. When I call for beef I typically want you to use rib eye or sirloin that is usually sliced paper-thin, which is something most butchers probably won't do for you unless they are both very nice and very patient. To do it at home, cut the steak into two pieces and put them in the freezer for an hour, or until they are almost frozen. Then, with a very sharp knife, almost shave the beef for several of the recipes in this book, such as *Hayashi Raisu* (page 144) and *Gyudon* (page 141). Ground beef (not the leanest) is used for dishes like *Menchi Katsu* (page 124).

MIRIN This sweetened rice wine (sweet cooking sake) is an essential Japanese flavoring. It imparts sweetness and good glazing properties to teriyaki sauce, is frequently added to simmered dishes, and is often used in place of sugar because it contributes a more complex sweetness. Sauces that include mirin are heated before using to cook off the alcohol taste and concentrate the flavor. I use a regular mirin made by Takara that has an alcohol content of about 12 percent. Other types of mirin include naturally brewed *hon mirin*, or "true mirin," which has a slightly higher alcohol content, and *aji mirin*, which is seasoned and is fine if that's what you can find.

MISO Japanese are passionate about this national food. There are many, many different types, but basically miso is a paste made from fermented soybeans, salt, rice or barley, and a starter culture.

If you can find different types (often named after the town where they were first made), try them to decide which type tastes best to you. Miso ranges from very light yellow, known as *shiro-miso* (*shiro* means "white") to a deep, rich brick-red brown, known as *aka-miso* (*aka* means "red"), with many variations in between. My family likes golden yellow *Shinshu miso* (named after my husband's home region). Most people just starting to eat miso favor *shiro-miso,* which is mild and almost sweet and is also the type most widely available outside of Asian markets. Although miso is high in sodium, it contains a lot of protein and nutrients and is considered a health food.

NAPA CABBAGE This elongated, pale green, ruffly leaved cabbage, known as *hakusai* in Japanese and sometimes called Chinese cabbage, has a milder taste than the green cabbage commonly used in Western cuisine. Remove any damaged outer leaves and then chop the cabbage for adding to stir-fries, *gyoza* fillings, simmered dishes, or soups. The Japanese never eat Napa cabbage raw, though it is a popular vegetable for pickling. I can find Napa cabbage at my usual market, but if you can't find it, use green cabbage (see Cabbage) or savoy cabbage.

NOODLES There is a huge variety of noodles in Japan, only some of which you will find at your local market. Japanese soba, udon, and ramen are all easily found outside of Japan.

There is no substitute for light brown soba noodles, made from a mix of buckwheat and wheat flours, especially when making cold soba (page 87). They have a nutty flavor and a firm texture and taste best when cooked al dente, drained, and rinsed in cold water immediately after cooking.

Popular at Japanese restaurants outside of Japan, thick, white udon noodles, made from wheat flour, are used in soups; added to hearty one-pot dishes such as *nabeyaki udon*, a rich, hot soup-stew with chicken, shrimp tempura, and vegetables; and sometimes eaten cold with a dipping sauce.

Best known as a quick, cheap dinner for college students and others, ramen has taken the world by storm. The thin, yellow wheat noodles are served both in broth and stir-fried. You can also eat them cold in *Hiyashi Chuka* (page 85). Believe it or not, for some of my ramen recipes, including *Miso Corn Bata Ramen* (page 92) and *Shohei no Butaniku to Goma Ramen* (page 91), if you must, you can use packaged instant ramen noodles (not the cup style) and just discard the flavor packet. Don't overcook them, as they will become mushy.

NORI Nori (also known as laver, a type of seaweed) is sold as plain pressed sheets and also toasted sheets (*yakinori*). The thin sheets of dark green (almost black) dried seaweed come in various grades and shapes,

from squares to shreds to rectangles that are perfectly sized for wrapping around a rice ball (see *Onigiri*, page 74). Nori is used for sushi, crumbled over rice, and shredded over cold noodle dishes, hot noodle soups, and even spaghetti.

Aonori (literally "blue nori"), a different type of seaweed, is sold dried and already crushed into small flakes, usually in a packet or a shaker. It has a very fresh marine aroma and, despite the translation, is medium green in color. It is sprinkled on dishes such as *Okonomiyaki* (page 30).

OILS In most recipes, I have specified canola oil or other neutral vegetable oil. By neutral I mean bland, so you might use safflower, corn, or another oil that has little or no flavor. I use canola oil for stir-frying as well as deep-frying because it gets hot without smoking, and it has no taste.

Toasted sesame oil *(goma abura)* is used in many Japanese recipes that have been adopted from the Chinese kitchen. It is primarily a seasoning oil, rather than a cooking oil. Rancidity can be a problem, so check the bottle for a sell-by date (not all bottles have them), and buy from markets with a high turnover. Once opened, store sesame oil in a cool, dark, dry place. Look for one hundred percent pure sesame oil. I use either Kadoya or Maruhon (Japanese brands).

Hot chili oil *(rayu)* is a popular condiment made by adding small red chili peppers to a neutral vegetable oil. It's great for jazzing up Chinese-inspired dishes like *Ebi no Chiri So-su* (page 107), *Mapo Dofu* (page 27) and ramen (pages 91–92). Many supermarkets carry chili oil.

OKONOMIYAKI SAUCE See Sauces.

PANKO Also called Japanese bread crumbs or honey-wheat bread crumbs, these light-colored, nearly flat shards of flaked wheat flour are used for many of the deep-fried recipes in this book, including *Tonkatsu* (page 110), *Ebi Furai* (page 102), and various *korokke* (croquettes). In fact, most fried foods in Japan, other than tempura, which uses a batter, are coated with *panko*, resulting in a light and very crispy coating.

Panko is readily available in plastic bags in the Asian or international foods section of supermarkets and is quite inexpensive. I usually repackage it in a freezer bag and store it in my freezer so I always have some on hand.

RAMEN NOODLES See Noodles.

RICE I could go on at length about the importance of rice to the Japanese diet and culture, about its history, the customs surrounding it, and the many different types available in Japan. But instead, I will simply say that nearly every Japanese home-style meal includes a bowl of rice. In the West, the rice you want is usually labeled Japanese or short grain. Never buy sweet rice, sometimes called glutinous rice, which is used mainly for *mochi* (rice cakes) and various other confections, or converted white rice, which lacks the proper texture.

Short-grain rice is stickier than long grain, which makes it easier to eat with chopsticks, and it can be found at almost any grocery. Short-grain brown rice, which still has the whole bran intact ("polishing" the bran from brown rice creates white rice), is available but is not popular in Japanese home kitchens because its strong taste and chewy texture interfere with other dishes. When I'm calling my family to the table at dinnertime, I always shout "*Gohan desu yo!*" which means "It's rice!" (For details on how to cook a good pot of rice, including the need to rinse, rinse, rinse, see page 73.)

RICE VINEGAR Milder than distilled white vinegar or white or red wine vinegar, rice vinegar *(komezu)* is the most common vinegar used in Japanese cooking. It is available at most markets, but be careful to buy plain rice vinegar, not sushi vinegar or seasoned rice vinegar.

It is a necessary ingredient in salad dressings and sauces, and it is also used for pickling and for preventing certain foods, such as apples and potatoes, from turning brown due to oxidation. My friends Hiroshi and Ikko each drink a tiny cup of *komezu* daily for their health because they believe it makes the blood strong.

SAKE Sake is for drinking and for cooking and is one of the key Japanese flavorings, along with soy sauce, mirin, dashi, and sugar. For cooking purposes, any inexpensive brand will do. It can even do for drinking, warmed in your microwave for about a minute. As with fine wines, there is a whole world of fine sake that I am not going to get into here. Just know that for cooking, the most basic sake will be fine, so buy the big bottle—it's inexpensive and keeps well in the pantry (no refrigeration necessary).

SAUCES See pages 16–17.

SESAME OIL See Oils.

SESAME SEEDS I use white sesame seeds. Black ones have a stronger sesame taste and are more visually exciting, but all the recipes in this book work fine with white. When buying sesame seeds, look for airtight packages and refrigerate the seeds in an airtight container after opening.

You will want to toast your sesame seeds; even if you have purchased seeds labeled roasted, they still need to be toasted to bring out the best flavor. To toast, heat a nonstick frying pan over medium-high heat. When the pan is hot, add the sesame seeds and heat, shaking the pan often to move the seeds around in it, until the seeds are golden and are releasing a heady sesame aroma, after only 3 to 4 minutes. Immediately pour the toasted seeds onto a plate to cool, as they can go quickly from nicely toasted to irretrievably burned.

SHICHIMI TOGARASHI & ICHIMI TOGARASHI

Shichimi means "seven flavors," and *togarashi* means "hot red pepper." *Shichimi togarashi* is a traditional spice mix made up of seven different peppers and other seasonings. Sometimes called seven-spice powder in English and also known as *nanami* in Japanese, it is great sprinkled into soups and on noodles, tempura, fried chicken, and more. Experiment—it's not too spicy but definitely adds

a nice little kick. You can find it at well-stocked supermarkets, at Asian groceries, and online. *Ichimi* means "one spice," so *ichimi togarashi* is simply finely ground hot red pepper. If you like spicy, this is the one for you.

SHIITAKE MUSHROOMS These mushrooms have been traditionally cultivated on the logs of the *shii* tree, hence the name (*take* means "mushroom"). They are meaty and dark brown with a strong mushroomy aroma and a smoky taste. Most of my recipes call for discarding the stems. You can buy the mushrooms fresh or dried (the dried ones have a stronger flavor). To reconstitute them, put them in very hot water for about 30 minutes or until softened, drain (you can save the soaking water for flavoring a soup base), blot dry with paper towels, remove and discard the stems, and then cut as directed in individual recipes for fresh mushrooms.

SOBA NOODLES See Noodles.

SOY SAUCE The most often used of all Japanese flavorings, soy sauce evokes much national pride. Naturally brewed from fermented soybeans, the sauce has a rich, yeasty, salty, deep flavor. Beware that there are pretenders to soy sauce out there that are not soy sauce at all, but rather chemical flavorings. I keep a large bottle of regular soy sauce in the refrigerator at all times. Kikkoman is a leading brand internationally and is widely available. Other types are sold, such as a lighter-colored soy sauce that some cooks use because it appears more attractive in certain dishes, as well as low-sodium and dark soy sauces. I use only regular soy sauce for the recipes in this book.

SUKIYAKI SAUCE See Sauces.

TERIYAKI SAUCE See Sauces.

TOFU In Japan, fresh tofu, immersed in water, is sold at local tofu shops, and it has a clean, taste and soft, almost creamy texture. The tofu available in the United States is reasonably good and inexpensive. In three basic types—firm, medium, and soft (silken, sometimes labeled *kinugoshi*)—tofu is sold in shelf-stable boxes that need to be drained and then refrigerated after opening or in plastic tubs that are refrigerated at the market. The tofu is usually, though not always, in a single large block, and the packages typically weigh 14 or 16 ounces. Always check the sell-by date on tofu packages. Once opened, tofu does not keep well and takes on the flavor of whatever is around it, so store it immersed in cold water in a clean, airtight container in the refrigerator, away from anything with a strong smell, for no more than a couple of days, changing the water daily.

TOMATO KETCHUP See Sauces.

TONKATSU SAUCE See Sauces.

TSUYU See Sauces.

TURNIP Small, white, mild-tasting Japanese turnips (*kabu*) are used for pickling and for adding to soups and stews. Since Western turnips are usually larger than the golf ball–size specimens stocked in Japanese markets, buy the smallest, blemish-free turnips available, and store them in a cool, dark place, if you can, because they become soggy if stored in the refrigerator for very long.

UDON NOODLES See Noodles.

WASABI This pungent green horseradish—no relation to Western horseradish—is a traditional condiment for sushi and is used in dipping sauces for noodles. It is available as a paste in tubes or as a powder in small cans. Once you open a tube, you must refrigerate it. To mix the powder, follow the package directions, which usually call for stirring together a small amount of the powder with a small amount of tepid water and letting it sit for a couple of minutes to allow the flavor to bloom. Be careful when you eat wasabi—a little dab packs a powerful punch.

WORCESTERSHIRE SAUCE See Sauces.

YAKISOBA SAUCE See Sauces.

Sources

ONLINE

www.japansuper.com

www.tokyocentral.com

www.japancentre.com

www.hmart.com

www.nijiyashop.com

HMart - Owned by a Korean company, these large, clean Asian supermarkets with locations in a number of states will have everything you need. You can also order online.

Mitsuwa - With locations in California and New Jersey, this is a full-service Japanese supermarket. No online ordering.

Nijiya - This full-service Japanese supermarket has an online store (a little hard to navigate), and locations in California, New York, and Hawaii.

99 Ranch - A chain of large, clean Chinese supermarkets, you can get everything you need here. Online ordering is available, and locations are in California, Washington, Nevada, and Texas.

Marukai - Their online shop is tokyocentral.com and store locations are in Southern California.

Wegmans, Whole Foods, King Soopers, Safeway, Kings, HEB, and Central Markets are among many regional and national supermarkets that carry a good variety of Japanese bottled sauces and packaged noodles, as well as tofu. Availability in these stores will vary by location.

Index

Let's Cook Japanese Food!

Produced by Weldon Owen, Inc.
A division of Bonnier Publishing USA

WELDON OWEN, INC.
President & Publisher Roger Shaw
SVP, Sales & Marketing Amy Kaneko
Finance & Operations Director Philip Paulick

Associate Publisher Amy Marr
Project Editor Alexis Mersel

Creative Director Kelly Booth
Art Director Marisa Kwek

Production Director Chris Hemesath
Associate Production Director Michelle Duggan
Imaging Manager Don Hill

Photographer Aubrie Pick
Food Stylist Lillian Kang
Prop Stylist Glenn Jenkins
Illustrator Putri Febriana

ACKNOWLEDGMENTS

Weldon Owen wishes to thank the following people
for their generous support in producing this book:
Lesley Bruynesteyn, Gloria Geller, Bessma Khalaf,
Veronica Laramie, Eve Lynch, and Elizabeth Parson.

A WELDON OWEN PRODUCTION
1045 Sansome Street, Suite 100
San Francisco, CA 94111
www.weldonowen.com

Printed and bound in China

First printed in 2016
10 9 8 7 6 5 4 3 2 1

Library of Congress Cataloging-
in-Publication data is available.

ISBN-13: 978-1-68188-177-5
ISBN-10: 1-68188-177-2

Additional photo credits
Shutterstock: pages 32–33, 154–155
Alamy: 128–129